JN084360

BRITISH NEWS UPDATE

5

Timothy Knowles
Minne Tanaka
Mihoko Nakamura
Sayaka Moue

KINSEIDO

Kinseido Publishing Co., Ltd.

3-21 Kanda Jimbo-cho, Chiyoda-ku,
Tokyo 101-0051, Japan

Copyright © 2023 by Timothy Knowles
                    Minne Tanaka
                    Mihoko Nakamura
                    Sayaka Moue

*All rights reserved. No part of this publication may
be reproduced, stored in a retrieval system, or transmitted,
in any form or by any means, electronic, mechanical,
photocopying, recording or otherwise, without the prior
permission of the publisher.*

First published 2023 by Kinseido Publishing Co., Ltd.

News clips ©BBC 2022.
Images ©BBC 2022.
Cover images ©BBC 2022.

This edition produced under license by Kinseido Publishing Co., Ltd. 2023.

BBC ニュース ホームページ：www.bbc.com/news

The British Broadcasting Corporation (BBC) is internationally famous for the quality and impartiality of its news items. BBC reporters also strive to make the news both interesting and as easy to understand as possible. In this book we have chosen 15 items that we think would be of particular interest, and therefore motivating. They are all about Britain, as you might expect, and learners will gain an insight into the life and culture of that country. However, most of the issues covered, such as health and education, are also important in Japan, so there is the opportunity to discuss and compare the two countries.

In 2021, the coronavirus pandemic dominated British news, but now, in Britain at least, Covid-19 is largely under control, However, you may notice that some of the videos were made under lockdown conditions, with people keeping a distance from each other. Also, as is discussed in one of the units, there are still some long-term concerns about the effects of the virus. The main topic, as in many previous years is the environment, and in particular, climate change: its effects, and efforts to either avoid it or deal with it. It's clear that both Japan and Britain are taking important steps to protect the futures of both our countries and the whole world.

As ever, new items of vocabulary are explained, and the notes (in Japanese) will explain any interesting points of grammar and usage of English. However the most important purpose of this book is that the learners should be able to engage in the subject matter, research, and then discuss together. With this in mind, we have developed discussion questions that would encourage them to relate these new discoveries with what is already familiar to them.

The videos are easily accessible online. This will make it easy for students to study by themselves out of class.

We hope you enjoy the book and the videos.

はじめに

　本書は、実際に放送された BBC（英国放送協会）のニュースを教材として、ニュースキャスターや街頭インタヴューを受ける native speaker が自然に話す英語に触れることで、学習者のリスニング力や語彙力といった英語力を伸ばすことを目的としています。同時に、イギリスや世界で起こっている出来事やその背景となる社会や文化についても学べるように工夫されています。

　扱うトピックは、政治、経済、環境などから、昨今世界中で猛威を振るっている新型コロナウイルス関連まで多岐にわたるものとし、できるだけ up to date でありつつも普遍的なものを選びました。学習する皆様の興味関心の幅を広げ、ご希望にお応えすることができれば幸いです。

　前作に引き続き、ユニット内のコラムは、イギリス文化についての興味深い情報を増やして充実を図り、Questions も最初の Setting the Scene に始まり Follow Up にいたるまで、各ユニットで取り上げるニュースを順序良く掘り下げて理解が深まるように配慮しました。

　本書を通じて、伝統と革新が共存する多民族国家イギリスが、4 つの地域の独自性を保ちつつ、総体としてのイギリスらしさ（"Britishness"）を模索する今の姿を見ていただけると思います。現在のイギリスは、新型コロナウイルスによる混乱は落ち着きつつありますが、3 人目の女性首相就任の直後に、70 年間にわたって国民を導いてきたエリザベス 2 世が 96 歳で崩御するなど、新たな時代を迎えています。日本や世界に与える影響を考慮すると、今後もその動きから目が離せません。

　このテキストを使って学習する皆様が、イギリスや世界の状勢に興味を持ち、さらには、自分から英語ニュースに触れたり、英語で意見を述べたりと、ますます学習の場が広がっていきますことを、執筆者一同願っております。

テキストの特徴

　普段の生活の中で、ニュースの英語に触れる機会はあまりないかもしれません。本テキストは、初めて英語でニュースを観る場合でも無理なく取り組めるよう、多種多様なアクティビティを用意しています。単語のチェックや内容確認、穴埋め、要約、ディスカッションを通して、段階を踏みながらニュースを理解できるような作りになっているので、達成感を感じることができるでしょう。

STARTING OFF

Setting the Scene

　実際にニュースを観る前に、ニュースで扱われるトピックについて考えるためのセクションです。トピックについての学習を始めるにあたり、身近な問題としてトピックを捉えられるような問題を用意しました。ここで先にニュースに関する情報を整理しておけば、実際にニュースを観る際に理解が容易になります。ニュースで使われている単語や語句、または重要な概念をここで予習しておきましょう。

Building Language

　ニュースの中で使われる重要単語を学びます。単に日本語の訳語を覚えるのではなく、英語での定義を通して、また同義語を覚えながら、単語の持つ意味を英語で理解することを目指します。また、これらの単語はディスカッションを行うときにもおそらく頻繁に使うことになる単語ですし、ニュースの核となる単語ですので、発音もしっかりと確認することが重要です。

WATCHING THE NEWS

Understanding Check 1

　実際にニュースの中身を詳しく見ていく前に、どんな意見が交わされているのかを確認します。ここで具体的にニュースのイメージをつかむことが大事です。全体像を簡単にでも把握することで、ニュース理解の大きな助けとなります。

Understanding Check 2

　ニュースに関する問題を解くことで、どれだけニュースを理解できたか確認することができます。間違えた箇所に関しては、なぜ間違えたのかをしっかりと分析し、内容を正確に把握しましょう。**Filling Gaps** のアクティビティを行ってから **Understanding Check 2** に取り組むのも効果的かもしれません。

Filling Gaps

　ニュースの中で重要な意味を持つ単語を聞き取ります。何度も繰り返し聞き、正しい発音を意識します。それと同時に、単語を正しく書き取ることで、耳と手との両方の動きを通して重要単語を習得することを目指します。もし時間に余裕があれば、穴埋めの単語を実際に発音し、耳と手に加え口も使って覚えると効果的です。

MOVING ON

Making a Summary

　この箇所は、これまで観てきたニュースをまとめる部分でもあり、かつ **Follow Up** に至る前の準備の段階でもあります。しっかりと内容を理解しているか、このアクティビティを通して確認しましょう。また、**Building Language** で出てきた単語を再度使っているため、単語の習熟の確認ができるようになっています。

Follow Up

　ニュースと関連したトピックをいくつか挙げてあります。ニュースで得た知識、また単語を活かして話し合いを行うためのセクションです。トピックには、その場で話し合えるものと各自調べてから発表し合うもの、両方が含まれています。そのニュースに関してだけでなく、今後似たような話題に接したときにも意見を述べることができるよう、このアクティビティで仕上げを行います。

Background Information

　ニュースでは、必ずしもすべての事柄が説明されているとは限りません。ニュースの核となる事柄で、かつニュースの中ではあまり詳しく説明されていないことに関して、このセクションでは補足しています。ニュースをより深く理解するのにも役立ちますし、**Follow Up** での話し合いの際にも使えるかもしれません。

Behind the Scenes

　ニュースに関連することではありますが、**Background Information** とは異なりここではニュースの核となることではなく、話題が広がる知識、教養が深まる知識を取り上げました。肩の力を抜き、楽しんで読めるような内容になっています。

・各ユニットで取り上げたニュース映像はオンラインで視聴することができます。詳しくは巻末を参照ください。

・テキスト準拠の Audio CD には、各ユニットのニュース音声と、ニュースを学習用に聞き取りやすく吹き替えた音声、Making a Summary を収録しています。

Contents

Map of The United Kingdom

正式名称は **The United Kingdom of Great Britain and Northern Ireland**（グレートブリテ
ン及び北アイルランド連合王国）。**England**（イングランド）、**Wales**（ウェールズ）、**Scotland**（ス
コットランド）、**Northern Ireland**（北アイルランド）の4国から成る連合国家です（2022年現在）。

※（　）は本テキストでその地名、場所が登場
　するユニットを表します

Greater London

North Atlantic Ocean

Inverness

Scotland

North
Sea

Glasgow

Edinburgh

Mayfair
(Unit 9)　**Westminster**
(Unit 8)　**Victoria Park**
(Unit 2)

Hounslow
(Unit 3)　**Hanwell**
(Unit 3)

River Thames

Heathrow
(Unit 3)

Shoreditch
(Unit 12)

Lambeth
(Unit 12)

Newcastle
(upon Tyne)

Northern
Ireland

Isle of Man

Belfast

York

Irish Sea

Liverpool

Manchester

Ireland

Conwy

Stoke (Unit 14)

Wales

Birmingham

England

Cambridge

Cardiff

Oxford

Rochford
(Unit 7)

Surrey
(Unit 11)

Dover

Cornwall
(Unit 5)

Portsmouth

Canterbury Cathedral
(Unit 1)

St. Ives

Plymouth

Brixham
(Unit 7)

Isle of Wight

Kingsbridge
(Unit 7)

Unit 1

The Windows of Canterbury Cathedral

最新の技術により、いにしえの人工物の研究が進んでいます。イギリスへのキリスト教伝道の発祥地の１つであり、イギリス国教会総本山でもあるカンタベリーで、どのような発見があったのでしょうか。ニュースを見てみましょう。

On Air Date   26 July 2021

STARTING OFF

Setting the Scene

What do you think?

1. What is the oldest building that you have been to? Where is it, how old is it, and what did you think about it?

2. How do we know the age of buildings, and things in those buildings?

3. Is it important to know how old things are?

Building Language

For each word (1-6), find two synonyms (a-l).

1. stunning　　　[　][　]

2. assassination　[　][　]

3. feature　　　[　][　]

4. witness　　　[　][　]

5. conflagration　[　][　]

6. perspective　　[　][　]

a. be highlighted	g. viewpoint
b. outlook	h. astonishing
c. appear	i. impressive
d. see	j. inferno
e. murder	k. observe
f. killing	l. blaze

WATCHING THE NEWS

Understanding Check 1

Read the quotes, then watch the news and match them to the right people.

a. ... putting all the pieces in place, and then we finally get an answer, something new ...

b. The cathedral authority say it's a hugely significant find, ...

c. These are all stories that were recorded at the time they happened here.

d. For decades, historians have thought that some of these panels were made earlier than the others ...

( )   ( )   ( )   ( )

Understanding Check 2

Which is the best answer?

1. What have scientists discovered about the stained-glass windows?

   a. They were all made in the 13th century.

   b. Some of them might have been made in the mid-1100s.

   c. There are many different styles.

   d. They are not as old as the scientists thought they might be.

2. What is special about the "windolyser"?

   a. We can work out the age of glass without damaging it.

   b. The beam causes the surface of glass to radiate.

   c. It doesn't leave chemical fingerprints.

   d. It was developed by scientists while on location.

3. Which of the following historical events was <u>not</u> mentioned?

   a. A great fire destroyed the cathedral.

   b. Thomas Becket was assassinated.

   c. King Charles I was executed.

   d. King Henry II begged for forgiveness.

What do you remember?

4. What is special about Canterbury Cathedral?

_____

5. According to the male researcher, what kind of story have they been working on, and why does he think the answer is fantastic?

_____

6. According to the reporter, Pallab Ghosh, what has this scientific discovery given us?

_____

Background Information

　ケント州にあるカンタベリー大聖堂 (Canterbury Cathedral) はイングランド国教会の総本山で、ユネスコ世界遺産にも登録されている由緒ある教会です。597 年、ローマより、初のカンタベリー大司教 (the Archbishop of Canterbury) となる聖アウグスティヌス (St Augustine) がサクソン人の支配下にあったこの地を訪れ、最初の大聖堂を設立しました。その後、ノルマン征服 (the Norman Conquest) の翌年となる 1067 年に火災で建物が破壊されると、1070 年から 77 年にかけてノルマン様式での全面的な建て直しが行われました。また、1174 年に大火が起きた際には、新たにゴシック様式の建物が追加されるなどして再建されました。以後、度々増改築が繰り返された結果、現在見ることのできる荘厳な大聖堂の姿となりました。

　ニュースで取り上げられているステンドグラスは「祖先シリーズ (Ancestors Series)」と呼ばれる、キリストの祖先の肖像を描いた 86 枚の作品の一部です。このシリーズは当初、1174 年の大火の後から 1220 年にかけて、再建計画の一環として徐々に制作されたとみられていました。しかし 1980 年代になると、美術史家のマデリン・H・キャヴィネス (Madeline H. Caviness, 1938-) の指摘により、13 世紀に設置されたとされる 4 枚のパネルが、様式から判断してもっと古い時代に作られたのではないかと推測されるようになりました。この説を検証すべく、ユニバーシティ・カレッジ・ロンドンの研究チームが今回の調査を行いました。チームは対象を破壊することなく化学分析できるポータブル蛍光エックス線 (pXRF: portable x-ray fluorescence) 分析計を使用し、3D プリンタで作った独自の装置である「ウィンドライザー (windolyser)」を取り付けて、これらのステンドグラスを調査しました。その結果、いくつかの作品において、他の 13 世紀に作られたとされるパネルよりも古い年代のガラスが使われていることが判明しました。このことから、これらの作品は大火が起きる前に制作され、焼失を免れて、大聖堂再建の際に今ある場所に設置されたのではないかと推測されています。

　同チームはカンタベリー大聖堂だけでなくヨーク大聖堂 (York Minster) のステンドグラスについても同様に調査し、制作者や年代の特定を行いました。今後も何か発見があるかもしれません。

参考
https://www.canterbury-cathedral.org/heritage/history/cathedral-history-in-a-nutshell/
https://www.ucl.ac.uk/news/2021/jul/stained-glass-present-murder-thomas-becket-could-be-oldest-existing-england

Filling Gaps

CD 1-02 ORIGINAL   CD 1-03 VOICED

Watch the news, then fill the gaps in the text.

Newsreader: Canterbury Cathedral, a place of Christian worship for over a thousand years is now believed to be the home of some of the oldest examples of stained glass anywhere in the world. Er, some panels have now been redated using a new (¹   ), and experts say they were crafted in the middle of the twelfth century. The cathedral authority

5   say it's a hugely significant find, as very little was thought to have (²   ) from the fabric of the early cathedral, as our science correspondent Pallab Ghosh reports.

Pallab Ghosh: Canterbury Cathedral is among the oldest churches in England. Inside, its (³   ) windows (⁴   ) symbolic religious scenes. This series was thought to have been made in the 13th century. But some of the panels, including

10   this one of the prophet Nathan, have now been (⁵   ).

Ghosh: For decades, historians have thought that some of these panels were made earlier than the others because they're different in (⁶   ). Now, using a new technique, scientists have (⁷   ) that not only are they much older, but they may well be among the oldest in the world.

15 **Ghosh:** It's only come to light now because of this (⁸   ) called a "windolyser". It may not look like much, but it was developed by scientists to be used on location,

20   without damaging the glass.

Ghosh: It shines a beam onto the (⁹   ) which causes the material inside to radiate. This radiation contains a chemical fingerprint from which the researchers worked out its age.

Professor Ian Freestone, the UCL Institute of Archaeology: We've been working on

25   this (¹⁰   ) (¹¹   ), for some time, putting all the pieces in place, and then we finally get an answer, something new, that brings together science and

4

art into one story. It's fantastic.

Léonie Seliger, Stained Glass Conservation, Canterbury Cathedral: These are all
stories that were recorded at the time they happened here.

Ghosh: The discovery has astonished
Léonie Seliger who looks after the
stained-glass windows here. She
believes that the redated panels could
go back to the mid-1100s, and were
(^{12}) (^{13})

during great historical events at the cathedral, including the (^{14})
of the then archbishop, Thomas Becket, who (^{15}) in many of these
windows.

Seliger: They would have (^{16}) the murder of Thomas Becket. They would
have (^{17}) Henry II come on his knees begging for forgiveness.
They would have (^{18}) the (^{19}) of the fire that
devoured the cathedral in 1174. Um, and then they would have (^{20})
all of British history.

Ghosh: The cathedral contains the story of England's history, its artistry, and its religious
thinking. Now, a new scientific discovery has given us a fresh (^{21})
on the nation's past. Pallab Ghosh, BBC News, Canterbury Cathedral.

Notes

ℓ1 **Canterbury Cathedral**「カンタベリー大聖堂」イングランド南東部ケント州東部の都市カンタベリーにある大聖堂。ヨーク大聖堂と並ぶイングランド国教会総本山の1つ　ℓ10 **the prophet Nathan**「預言者ナタン」旧約聖書に描かれるダビデ王の顧問役の預言者　ℓ24 **the UCL Institute of Archaeology**「UCL 考古学研究所」イギリス有数の規模を誇る考古学研究所。UCL はユニバーシティ・カレッジ・ロンドン (University College London) の略称。ロンドン大学最大のカレッジで、1827 年創設　ℓ37 **Thomas Becket**「トマス・ベケット (1118?-70)」イングランドの聖職者。国王ヘンリー 2 世の下で大法官 (1155-62) とカンタベリー大司教 (1162-70) を務めた。王と対立し、王の言葉を曲解した部下により、カンタベリー大聖堂内で殺害された。T・S・エリオット (T. S. Eliot, 1888-1965) の『寺院の殺人』(*Murder in the Cathedral*, 1935) にその様子が描かれている　ℓ40 **Henry II**「ヘンリー 2 世 (1133-89)」イングランド国王。在位 1154-89。自らの言葉によってトマス・ベケットの死を招いたことを知り、カンタベリー大聖堂でひざまずいて許しを請うた

『カンタベリー物語』

　1170 年の死後、トマス・ベケットは神格化され、カンタベリー大聖堂は一大巡礼地として多くの巡礼者が訪れることになりました。ジェフリー・チョーサー (Geoffrey Chaucer, 1342/43-1400) が 14 世紀に著した『カンタベリー物語』(*The Canterbury Tales*) は、ベケットの聖廟があるカンタベリーに向かう巡礼者たちがロンドンのサザーク (Southwark) にある宿で一緒になるところから始まります。宿屋の主人ハリー・ベイリーによる提案で、旅の道中に全員が物語を語って誰の話が一番面白いかを競い合うことになり、騎士、粉屋、料理人、バースの女房、学僧、医者、免罪符売り、船長など、様々な身分、職業、性別の巡礼者が順番に語っていきます。語り手の階級や性別、テーマなどによって文体、韻律、スタイルにも変化が見られますが、多様な人々が入り混じる巡礼団という設定を用いることで、文学に精通したチョーサーによる様々なジャンルの物語が可能になっており、中英語 (Middle English) で書かれたこの作品は、イギリス文学において最も重要な作品のひとつとなっています。

MOVING ON

Making a Summary

 CD 1-04

Fill the gaps to complete the summary.

　Canterbury Cathedral is one of the oldest Christian (**c** 　　　　) in England. It is more than 1,000 years old, and contains (**s** 　　　　) stained-glass windows that (**d** 　　　) religious scenes. Up to now, they were thought to have been made in the 13th century, but a new (**t** 　　　　), using a (**d** 　　　　) called a "windolyser", confirms that some of them go back to the mid-1100s, and might be among the oldest in the world. This (**d** 　　　　) can be used on location without damaging the glass. It causes the inside material to radiate, with a chemical (**f** 　　　　) that indicates its age. According to the professor, this result is fantastic, as it joins science and art. The windows would have (**w** 　　　　) many historical events, such as the (**a** 　　　　　) of Thomas Becket, who (**f** 　　　　) in many of the windows, and even the (**c** 　　　　　) that destroyed the cathedral in 1174. This discovery has given us a fresh (**p** 　　　　) on England's past.

Follow Up

Discuss, write or present.

1. What buildings in Japan can you think of that might have witnessed some important historical events? Say something about them.

2. In the video we can see these huge, beautiful windows in the Cathedral. What do you think of them? Why did they put windows like this in the Cathedral?

3. Do you agree that the "windolyser" gives us a fresh perspective to a nation's past?

Unit 2

A Skateboarding School for Women

東京オリンピックで注目を浴びたスケートボードですが、イギリスでもオリンピックをきっかけにスケートボードを始める女性が増え、思わぬ効果を生み出しているようです。ニュースを見てみましょう。

On Air Date   25 August 2021

STARTING OFF

Setting the Scene

What do you think?

1. What do you think of skateboarding? Have you ever tried it? If so, how was it?

2. Do you think that skateboarding is an activity for women?

3. Did you watch skateboarding at the Tokyo Olympics? Do you think it should remain an Olympic sport?

Building Language

Which word or phrase (1-7) best fits which explanation (a-g)?

1. inspire   [   ]
2. confidence   [   ]
3. booming   [   ]
4. accelerate   [   ]
5. crack on   [   ]
6. buzz   [   ]
7. dominate   [   ]

a. cause greater activity or progress; go faster

b. the feeling that you can achieve something, and won't fail

c. encourage someone; give confidence and motivation to do something

d. be most important; control or rule over

e. keep going without giving up

f. very successful; flourishing

g. excitement; exhilaration

Understanding Check 1

Read the quotes, then watch the news and match them to the right people.

    a. It's really good to, like, focus on something and really concentrate on it.

    b. To find it, you just need to get on the board.

    c. It's really freeing, being able to, like, you feel like you're 100% in control.

    d. I got to a point where I'm like I need to share this with people.

  ( )   ( )   ( )   ( )

Understanding Check 2

Which is the best answer?

1. How long has Meg been skateboarding?
    a. about a month
    b. She just started today.
    c. about a week
    d. a few weeks

2. In what way does Lyndsay think that skateboarding is similar to life?
    a. If something bad happens, you keep going and don't give up.
    b. It's not so difficult to learn.
    c. Often you get so focused on something that you forget what you're doing.
    d. If you practise regularly, you will succeed.

3. Amber tells us why she loves skateboarding. What does she <u>not</u> mention?
    a. It's a great way to make friends.
    b. Skateboarding is good exercise and keeps her healthy.
    c. She likes being able to focus and concentrate on something.
    d. It has helped her with her mental problems.

What do you remember?

4. How did the Olympic Games affect skateboarding in London?

---

5. Why does Lyndsay want to teach women how to skateboard?

---

6. According to the reporter, Megan Lawton, how can we find the skateboarder in all of us?

Background Information

　新型コロナウィルス感染症のパンデミックのため、1年の延期を経て2021年に開催された東京オリンピックでは、スケートボードが新競技として加わりました。イギリスのオリンピック選手団では、スカイ・ブラウン（Sky Brown, 2008- ）とボンベット・マーチン（Bombette Martin, 2006- ）の2名の女子選手が出場しました。ブラウンは、夏のオリンピックではイギリスチーム史上最年少の13歳で競技に臨み、銅メダルを獲得しました。日本人の母親とイギリス人の父親の間に生まれたブラウンは宮崎県出身で、世界最年少のプロスケートボーダー、サーファーとして活動しています。

　パンデミックで数回のロックダウンを経験したイギリスでは、オリンピックの影響もあってスケートボードがかつてない人気を得ており、公園や駐車場で練習する人の姿が多く見られるようになりました。2020年には5万人強だった競技人口が、2021年にはほぼ2倍になり、10万人を超えました。家に籠りがちなロックダウン中、密を避けて身体を動かすことができ、ボード1枚で手軽に始められることが人気の要因です。バランスを保つ練習をしている初級者から、より高度な技を目指す上級者まで、技術に集中することでメンタル面も補強することができます。

　そんな中、イースト・ロンドンでは、女性のためのスケートボード教室が人気を集めています。ヴィクトリア・パークでリンジー・マクラーレン（Lyndsay McLaren）によって始められたネイバーフッド・スケート・クラブ（Neighbourhood Skate Club）は、あらゆる年齢や背景の女性が、スケートボードを通して交流し、やりたいことを実現して自信を持てるようになることを目標に活動しています。東京オリンピックの開会に合わせた集会では、2歳から42歳までの初心者が大集合しました。

参考
https://olympics.com/en/news/sky-brown-and-bombette-martin-on-team-gb-olympic-skateboarding-team
https://www.theguardian.com/lifeandstyle/2020/nov/22/lets-flip-again-skateboards-take-off-for-a-new-generation
https://surfgirlmag.com/2021/08/neighbourhood-skate-club-takes-over-victoria-park/

Filling Gaps

Watch the news, then fill the gaps in the text.

Newsreader: Well, a sport that had its (^{1}) at the Tokyo Olympics was of course skateboarding. It helped to make women on boards a more familiar sight, and has (^{2}) more Londoners to give it a go, including our reporter Megan Lawton, who's been to an East London park to find out more.

5   **Lyndsay McLaren:** So, my arm's here if you need it.

Meg: OK.

Megan Lawton: Until last week Meg hadn't been on a skateboard before, but she's now one of 60 women who

10   come for (^{3}) lessons in Victoria Park.

Meg: It's really freeing, being able to, like, you feel like you're 100% in control. Um, you're able to move, and obviously because it's so male (^{4}), a woman on a skateboard, it just, you feel like, so (^{5}).

15   **Lawton:** The group is run by Lyndsay McLaren, who (^{6}) to skate 10 years ago while studying in Miami.

McLaren: I want other women to be able to feel the (^{7}) and the joy that I feel when I'm skating. I got to a point where I'm like I need to share this with people. Um, I want, so, so many women have said to me like I wish, I wish I could do that. And

20   I'm like you can, you can do that too, you know.

Lawton: Neighbourhood's client list was already (^{8}) before skateboarding was included in this year's Olympics. But, it's (^{9}) things further, (^{10}) more women to pick up a board.

McLaren: When you're skating and you get super into it and you're really focused on

25   learning something new, or even just learning how to (^{11}), er, when

you fall you just pick yourself up and, and (^{12} _____) (^{13} _____) with

it, and I think that's something that's kind of like (^{14} _____) to, to life.

Lawton: Like Meg, Amber is also new to skating, and says it's way more than just a

(^{15} _____).

Amber: I love skateboarding because it's

helped me so much, um, with like

(^{16} _____) health

problems and stuff like that. It's really

good to, like, focus on something and

really concentrate on it. So, every

time I feel a little bit down it's really good to like get out, meet (^{17} _____)

of people and every one at the skateparks are super friendly, so I've really met some of

my really good friends through skateboarding.

Lawton: If you're sat at home thinking skateboarding isn't for me, I don't have the right skill

set, Lyndsay would say you're (^{18} _____), and there's a skateboarder in all of

us. To find it, you just need to get on the board.

Woman: You're doing it!

Lawton: It's safe to say I won't be (^{19} _____) Team GB in the Paris Olympics.

McLaren: OK, come, come.

Lawton: But that's not what this skate group are about. For them it's about the

(^{20} _____) of being on a board, and the friends you make through doing it.

Megan Lawton BBC London.

Newsreader: Good on Megan for having a go.

Notes

ℓ 11 **Victoria Park**「ヴィクトリア・パーク」イースト・ロンドンにある公園。1845 年開園。園内には 2011 年に開設されたスケートボード場がある　ℓ 16 **Miami**「マイアミ」アメリカ合衆国のフロリダ州にある都市　ℓ 21 **Neighbourhood (Skate Club)**「ネイバーフッド（・スケート・クラブ）」女性がスケートボードをする機会の向上を目指し、2021 年にリンジー・マクラーレンによって設立された　ℓ 43 **Team GB**「チーム GB」イギリスオリンピック委員会（British Olympic Association）が 1999 年からイギリスのオリンピック選手団に使用している名称。GB はグレート・ブリテン（Great Britain）の略称

スケートボードとサーフィン

　スカイ・ブラウン選手のように、スケートボードとサーフィンの両方を楽しんでいる人は少なくありません。そもそもスケートボードの始まりは、1950年代頃、カリフォルニア州のサーファーたちが波の無い時にも波乗りを体感できるよう、ローラースケートの車輪を取り付けた板に乗って陸上を走行したことでした。歩道 (sidewalk) を滑ることから「サイドウォーク・サーフィン (sidewalk surfing)」と呼ばれるようになったこのスポーツが徐々に人気となり、現在のスケートボードへと発展しました。1965年に世界初のスケートパークであるサーフ・シティ (Surf City) がアリゾナ州に誕生して以来、本場カリフォルニア、オーストラリア、カナダなど、アメリカ国内外に様々な趣向を凝らした施設が作られるようになりました。イギリスでも1978年、イースト・ロンドンにロム・スケートパーク (Rom Skatepark) がオープンし、2014年にはイギリス国内の重要建築物として2級指定建造物に登録されました。

MOVING ON

Making a Summary

 CD 1-07

Fill the gaps to complete the summary.

　The 2020 Tokyo Olympics (**i**　　　　　　) Londoners, especially women, to take up skateboarding. Lyndsay McLaren teaches a group of women in an East London park. She does it because she wants women to feel the same (**c**　　　　　) and joy that she does when skateboarding. If you fall, you just pick yourself up and (**c**　　　　　) (**o**　　　　　), which is transferable to life itself. Her company was already (**b**　　　　　) before, but the Olympics (**a**　　　　) things, as more women were (**i**　　　　) to try it. One woman said she did it because she felt in control and strong in a male (**d**　　　　) activity, and another said she loved it because it was good to meet friendly people and make friends through skateboarding. Lyndsay would say there's a skateboarder in all of us, and you just need to get on the board. The group is all about the (**b**　　　　) of being on a skateboard, and the friends you make.

Follow Up

Discuss, write or present.

1. What do you think of Lyndsay's suggestion that skateboarding is like life: when you fall you pick yourself up and crack on?

2. Each of the skateboarding pupils explained why they loved it. Think of an activity that you love – it doesn't have to be a sport – and try to explain to a partner why you love it.

3. Find out what the other new sports at the 2020 Olympics were. Also, what will be the new sports in 2024 (Paris) be? Do you think these sports should be in the Olympics?

Unit 3

West London's Community Gardens

新型コロナウィルスによるロックダウン以来ロンドンでは都市菜園が静かな人気を呼んでいますが、その実態はどのようなものでしょうか。ニュースを見てみましょう。

On Air Date   28 April 2021

STARTING OFF

Setting the Scene

What do you think?

1. What do you do to relax?

2. Have you ever done gardening?

3. Do you think that gardening is good for you, or is it just hard work?

Building Language

Which word or phrase (1-7) best fits which explanation (a-g)?

1. emerge   [   ]

2. connected   [   ]

3. flourish   [   ]

4. soothing   [   ]

5. dispose of   [   ]

6. horticultural [   ]

7. rolling   [   ]

a. to do with gardening, and cultivation of flowers, fruit and vegetables

b. started, in operation

c. succeed, prosper, be very healthy

d. having a calm, gentle effect that stops you worrying

e. come out to where you can be seen, perhaps from a difficult experience

f. feeling that you are with people, and not alone

g. get rid of, deal with

WATCHING THE NEWS

Understanding Check 1

Read the quotes, then watch the news and match them to the right people.

a. … I depend on it to get my kind of hands on, hands in the soil …

b. I think it really teaches them skills they can transfer for the rest of their life.

c. And it's community gardens like this, that are so important to Londoners.

d. All we need is another little push to get this site live …

( )   ( )   ( )   ( )

Understanding Check 2

Which is the best answer?

1. Where is the first garden that appeared in the video?

   a. near an oasis

   b. near an airport

   c. in a place where there is lots of access to outside space

   d. in a green space on a balcony

2. What do the people in the gardens do with their weeds?

   a. They make salads with them for their meals.

   b. They throw them in the garbage.

   c. They burn them.

   d. They feed them to the chickens.

3. Who can access, work and participate in these gardens?

   a. only local people

   b. only people who have passed their gardening test

   c. everyone who is willing to work there

   d. only people who have paid the correct fee

What do you remember?

4. How did the people in the gardens describe the experience? Try to remember as many adjectives and phrases as you can.

_____

5. According to the woman talking about the site at Hanwell, what do they need, and what do they need to do?

_____

6. According to the man at the end, what is the main benefit for people who participate in these gardens?

_____

Background Information

　イギリスのコミュニティ・ガーデンの歴史は古く、数百年にわたって人々の貴重な食糧供給源として機能してきました。特に第 2 次世界大戦においては戦時農園（victory garden）として市中の庭や公園などに数多くの菜園が建設され、そこで育てられた野菜や果物が地元の人々に供給されました。戦後、その数はいったん減少しますが、1960 年代後半になると都市の緑化への関心が高まりを見せるようになり、空き地を菜園や花園に変えるなどして多くのコミュニティ・ガーデンが造られるようになりました。

　新型コロナウイルスが世界的な流行を見せた 2020 年以降、その需要はさらに高まっています。都市のロックダウンによる食糧不安への懸念から、コミュニティ・ガーデンは食糧供給源として再び注目されるようになりました。また、外出制限や不安・ストレスなどによる身心の不調を訴える人が増加する中、土や草木に触れることで健康の回復を促す「園芸療法（horticultural therapy）」の手段としても期待されています。2020 年に行われたあるオンライン調査によると、回答者 2,400 人超のうち、庭や屋外スペースが健康にとって非常に重要であると感じている人は 92% で、ロックダウン中にこうした空間を利用することでストレスや不安を軽減する効果を得られた、と答えた人は 87% に上りました。

　自然との触れ合いや地域の人々とのつながりがもたらす健康効果には、国民保健サービス（NHS: National Health Service）も着目しています。NHS では身体的または精神的な疾患を抱える患者に対し、地域での活動を通じて症状の改善を促す「社会的処方（social prescribing）」を拡大することを掲げており、地元の人々と自然の中を散歩したり、園芸や畑仕事に従事したりすることによる健康への効果を見込んでいます。こうした「緑の社会的処方（green social prescribing）」に対し、イギリス政府は 2020 年、400 万ポンド（約 6 億円、1 ポンド＝150 円）を出資することを発表しました。EU 離脱（Brexit）やパンデミックによる社会の混乱が長引く中、コミュニティ・ガーデンが育むつながりの大切さが見直されています。

参考
https://www.bbc.co.uk/gardening/today_in_your_garden/community_about.shtml
https://ruaf.org/news/covid-19-a-growing-opportunity-for-community-gardening-in-london/
https://ngs.org.uk/new-report-gardens-and-coronavirus-2020/
https://www.england.nhs.uk/personalisedcare/social-prescribing/green-social-prescribing/

Watch the news, then fill the gaps in the text.

Newsreader: Now, if you're lucky enough to have a garden or a balcony, you might have

found time during lockdown to enjoy your green space a little more than usual. And as

we (^{1}) from the pandemic, nature, and being outside, is helping some

Londoners feel a bit more (^{2}). Wendy Hurrell spent the day in a

5 garden which is helping the community (^{3}).

Wendy Hurrell: By a busy main road beneath Heathrow's flightpath, this is Hounslow, in

West London, a (^{4}) populated area where people have limited

(^{5}) to outside space. But, there's a secret oasis here. And it's

community gardens like this, that are so important to Londoners.

10 **Hurrell:** A place for calm, learning, and growing. The Salopian Garden is open to anyone who

wants to get their hands (^{6}).

Hurrell: So let's go and meet the volunteers.

Hurrell: This group is called 'Soup for Lunch'. Today they're planting melons in the peace of

the polytunnel.

15 **First woman:** You wouldn't think you were just off of the main road, would you? It's

unbelievable. Yeah, it's lovely. Yeah, we're all (^{7}) *(laughing)*.

Hurrell: Jaz learns tips here that she takes home to her husband and their own garden.

Jaz: We gradually build it up with, um, through plants from here and, from here, some from

here as well.

20 **Hurrell:** It's tremendously (^{8}) to see it grow like that.

Jaz: Yes it's, it's relaxing and you sit out there and you see the flowers and the vegetables. And

it's sort of, I don't know, out of this world, I think *(laughing)*.

Hurrell: Do you have a garden where you live, or is this your garden?

Second woman: This is my garden. Yeah, not, not even a balcony so, um, I depend on it to

25 get my kind of hands on, hands in the soil, it's, it's, it's (^{9}). I don't

know, it's the smells, it's the (^{10}).

Hurrell: Not even the unwanted plants go to waste.

Hurrell: They have an excellent way of (^{11}) (^{12}) weeds here. Here you go girls. There's some dandelion leaves. Yum, yum.

Hurrell: The pandemic means restrictions on numbers here, but school groups and (^{13}) training will resume.

Hurrell: This garden has been (^{14}) successful over the last ten years and there's another site Cultivate London has plans for. They're crowdfunding to turn this plot in Hanwell into a (^{15}) hub for young people.

Sylvia Cordell, Cultivate London: The funding platform is Spacehive, DIG Hanwell. All we need is another little push to get this site live, (^{16}) (^{17}) (^{18}) and get the community in here. And, and let's get working. We need our green spaces, we need to fight to keep them, and keep them open and (^{19}) to everyone.

Man: I think it really teaches them skills they can transfer for the rest of their life. There's a load of different paths with (^{20}), and to get into education and community kitchen gardens, therapy gardens.

Hurrell: They will tell you gardening is therapy. And in this community, it's for fun or even a full-time career. Wendy Hurrell, BBC London.

30

35

40

45

Notes

ℓ6 **Heathrow**「ヒースロー」大ロンドン地区西部にあるヒースロー空港（Heathrow Airport）のこと　ℓ6 **Hounslow**「ハウンズロー」大ロンドン地区西部のテムズ川沿いの地域。ヒースロー空港に隣接している　ℓ10 **The Salopian Garden**「サロピアン・ガーデン」ハウンズロー地域の公共菜園。カルティベート・ロンドンが 2016 年に開設　ℓ33 **Cultivate London**「カルティベート・ロンドン」アクトンに本拠地を置く慈善団体。都市園芸の普及と教育のため、2010 年に設立された　ℓ35 **Hanwell**「ハンウェル」ロンドン西部イーリング地区にある地域　ℓ39 **Spacehive**「スペースハイヴ」地域振興基金のためのクラウドファンドのプラットフォーム　ℓ39 **DIG Hanwell**「ディグ・ハンウェル」ハンウェル地域の菜園開設のためのクラウドファンド

イギリス王室の有機農業

　皇太子時代の国王チャールズ3世 (Charles III, 1948-) は農園を経営してきたことで知られています。1986年、テットベリー (Tetbury) にあるコーンウォール公領 (Duchy of Cornwall) の農園 (Duchy Home Farm) で、当時はまだ普及していなかった有機農業を全面的に取り入れました。彼は約1,000エーカー (4.046 km²) あるその農園で収穫した野菜や果物を販売するとともに、1990年に会社を立ち上げ、ダッチー・オリジナルズ (Duchy Originals、現在は Waitrose Duchy Organic) というブランド名でオーガニック食品の販売を開始し、その収益を全て慈善事業に充てました。2021年の農園の契約更新に先立ち、国王になる見込みだったチャールズ皇太子は、以後契約を更新せず、民間の有機農家に事業を引き継ぐことを発表しました。しかし、父フィリップ公 (Prince Philip, Duke of Edinburgh, 1921-2021) から2017年に受け継いだ王室所有の土地サンドリンガム (Sandringham) にあるウッド・ファーム (Wood Farm) でも新たに有機農業を開始し、これからも農業を続ける計画です。

MOVING ON

Making a Summary

 CD 1-10

Fill the gaps to complete the summary.

　As Londoners (**e** ⎯⎯⎯⎯⎯⎯) from the pandemic, nature is helping them feel more (**c** ⎯⎯⎯⎯⎯⎯). We are introduced to two natural sites that are helping the community (**f** ⎯⎯⎯⎯⎯⎯). The first is by a busy road in Hounslow, beneath the (**f** ⎯⎯⎯⎯⎯⎯) of Heathrow Airport. It has been very successful, and is open to anyone who wants to get their hands dirty. We are introduced to a local group called 'Soup for Lunch', who are planting melons in a (**p** ⎯⎯⎯⎯⎯⎯). Jaz learns tips she takes home to her own garden. She finds it relaxing and out of this world. Another woman has no garden at home, but finds it (**s** ⎯⎯⎯⎯⎯⎯) to put her hands in the soil. They (**d** ⎯⎯⎯⎯⎯⎯) of some of their weeds by feeding them to the chickens. The second site is in Hanwell, and they are hoping that crowdfunding will help to get it (**r** ⎯⎯⎯⎯⎯⎯) as a (**h** ⎯⎯⎯⎯⎯⎯) hub for young people. A woman from Cultivate London said that they need to fight to keep these green spaces open and accessible to everyone, and a man said it teaches them skills for their future careers.

Follow Up

Discuss, write or present.

1. The woman at the end thinks that green spaces are so important that they must fight to keep them and keep them open for everyone. Do you agree?

2. Are there places like this in Japanese cities where anybody can do some gardening?

3. If you had a small piece of land, what would you do with it? Would you grow plants, rear animals, or leave it as an open space?

Unit 4

Two Generations Sharing a Home

近年シェアハウスが人気ですが、イギリスで
は、同世代の友人同士での暮らしとは一味違
う「異世代ホームシェア」が注目を集めてい
ます。一体どのようなものなのでしょうか。
ニュースを見てみましょう。

On Air Date 15 August 2021

STARTING OFF

Setting the Scene

What do you think?

1. When you leave home and try to live by yourself, what sort of place would you look for? If you already live by yourself, what sort of place do you have?

2. One big problem for young people is finding a place that is not too expensive. Can you think of any solutions to this problem?

3. What sort of person would you like to share a flat with?

Building Language

For each word (1-7), find two synonyms (a-n).

1. spare   [   ][   ]
2. affordable   [   ][   ]
3. literal   [   ][   ]
4. virtual   [   ][   ]
5. vet   [   ][   ]
6. retain   [   ][   ]
7. standard   [   ][   ]

a. investigate	h. unused
b. economical	i. true
c. actual	j. normal
d. typical	k. hold
e. cheap	l. pretend
f. extra	m. check
g. keep	n. unreal

Understanding Check 1

Read the quotes, then watch the news and match them to the right people.

    a. I always say he speaks like Shakespeare to me …

    b. It's described as a homeshare arrangement for people …

    c. The benefit for them is really clear …

    d. Ah, sometimes when I'm on my bicycle, I feel half my age.

( )   ( )   ( )   ( )

Understanding Check 2

Which is the best answer?

1. Which of the following best describes the work of Two Generations?

    a. Its main aim is to promote friendship between the elderly.

    b. It helps elderly and disabled people to find accommodation.

    c. It reduces loneliness by inviting old people into young people's homes.

    d. It helps the elderly to share their homes with young people who need accommodation.

2. Which of the following sentences about George and Norman is correct?

    a. George is over 90, but Norman is much younger.

    b. Norman's wife has passed away, and George's family lives far away.

    c. Both George and Norman are studying at King's College.

    d. Norman met George in Syria.

3. The woman explained the benefits of the scheme for elderly people. Which of the following did she <u>not</u> mention?

    a. They can make a little of extra money to help them with their budget.

    b. They can retain their independence.

    c. They can feel safe because there is somebody else in their house at night.

    d. They don't have to move into a residential home.

What do you remember?

4. How does Norman feel when he is on his bicycle?

_____

5. Before George moved in with Norman, what did they have to do?

_____

6. Why does George think Norman speaks like Shakespeare to him?

_____

Background Information

　イギリスでは高齢化が急速に進んでおり、政府によれば 2019 年における 65 歳以上の高齢者の数は人口の 19% にあたる約 1,230 万人です。2009 年から 2019 年の間で全人口は 7% しか増加していないのに対し、65 歳以上は 23% 増加しています。高齢者の割合はこれからも増え続けると言われており、2043 年までに全人口の 24% にあたる 1,740 万人になると予測されています。

　こうした状況に伴い、高齢者の住宅事情も議論の対象になりつつあります。住宅・コミュニティ・地方自治省 (Ministry of Housing, Communities and Local Government) が 2018 年から 2019 年にかけて行った調査によれば、イギリス国内で 65 歳以上が世帯主の家は全体の 29% にあたる 690 万戸あり、そのうち持ち家に住む人は高齢者の 79% にあたる 542 万人です。また、65 歳以上の 45% が独り暮らしをしています。多くの高齢者の家では部屋が余っており、55% の高齢者世帯において 2 部屋以上の空き部屋があるというデータもあります。大きすぎる家に高齢者が住み続けるのにはメンテナンスなどの困難が伴う一方、住み慣れた場所から引っ越しをするにも障壁があり、高齢者の住宅問題はこれからさらに深刻さを増す見込みです。

　ホームシェアとは、高齢者や障がい者などといった、自分の持ち家で独立した生活を送るのに助けが必要な人と、家事などのサポートを提供する代わりに低料金で部屋に住みたい人をマッチングするプログラムで、1970 年代にアメリカで始まり、イギリスでは 1993 年に正式に開始されました。ホームシェアの支援組織であるホームシェア UK (Homeshare UK) によれば、2020 年は新型コロナウイルス感染症の影響で中断されたホームシェアも多かったものの、累計で 17 万 8,000 時間のサポートが 1,072 人の高齢者や障がい者に対して行われました。

　現在、ホームシェア UK には 20 団体が所属しており、その 1 つが今回のニュースで紹介されているツー・ジェネレーションズ (Two Generations) です。ツー・ジェネレーションズは 2018 年に設立され、好み、性別、文化、生活スタイル、趣味などに基づいて、高齢者などの部屋を提供する側と手伝いを提供する若者をマッチングします。サポートを提供する側の条件は、①21 歳以上であること、②イギリスに滞在する権利を有すること、③状況に応じて 10 時間から 20 時間のサポートを行うこと、④最低でも半年、理想的には 1 年参加すること、⑤2 人の身元保証人を立てること、⑥前歴開示および前歴者就業制限機構 (DBS: Disclosure and Barring Service) のチェックを受けることです。マッチングが完了すると、部屋の提供者は月 99 ポンド（約 1 万 5,000 円、1 ポンド＝150 円）を団体に支払い、手伝いを提供する側は、サポートの内容に従って約 249 ポンドから 299 ポンド（約 3 万 5,000 円から 4 万 2,000 円）を団体に支払います。家を提供する側は家事などを助けてもらい、サポートを提供する側は低料金で部屋を借りられるというお互いに利益となるプログラムになっており、何よりもお互いが社交的に生活し、独り暮らしによる孤独を解消する助けとなっています。

参考
https://homeshareuk.org/
https://twogenerations.co.uk/

Watch the news, then fill the gaps in the text.

Newsreader: It's described as a homeshare arrangement for people with a

(¹   ) room. Two Generations matches the (²   ) and

(³   ) with young people in need of accommodation. Well, it's seen an

(⁴   ) in requests since the start of the pandemic. The aim is to reduce

5   (⁵   ), but it's also built friendships, as Ayshea Buksh found out.

Ayshea Buksh: How old are you sir?

Norman: Ninety-three and a half.

Buksh: And how old do you feel?

Norman: Well, it depends. At the moment I'm feeling sort of 90ish. Ah, sometimes when I'm

10   on my bicycle, I feel half my age.

Norman: These are fuchsias.

Buksh: Norman may be a youthful

93-year-old. But he still

(⁶   ) needs a

15   helping hand from his flatmate,

George.

George: I prefer if I cook it from fresh.

Buksh: After his wife died, he lived (⁷   ) (⁸   )

(⁹   ) for several years. And George, who left his home in Syria to study

20   at King's College, needed an (¹⁰   ) place to live.

George: I lost a family, like, of course, I talk to them every day but it's impossible for me to

see them. So, I (¹¹   ) feel that I don't have a family except for

(¹²   ), so I get the sense of a family here.

Buksh: Both (¹³   ) (¹⁴   ) to a homeshare company which

25   matches young people with elderly or disabled individuals. They're heavily

(¹⁵   ) and security checked and must commit to at least six months or a year. But for Norman and George, the arrangements have (**16**   ) much

longer.

Natasha Langleben, Two Generations: The benefit for them is really clear, that they can

(**17**   ) their independence, remain in their home, they don't need to

make a (**18**   ) to move into a residential home if that's not what they

want. They don't, might not need a full-time carer, but they get that

(**19**   ) of mind that comes with overnight (**20**   ) and

the independence to remain at home.

Norman: George gets free accommodation. Er, I get (**21**   ) when I need it.

George: I always say he speaks like Shakespeare to me because he uses English that's

(**22**   ) English, so I

learn from him. I always ask about

the words.

Norman: His English is getting really very

good.

George: Thank you. But that's because of

his help, of course (*laughing*).

Buksh: Norman and George say they're both looking (**23**   ) to getting out

and about more, and enjoying the summer together. Ayshea Buksh, BBC London.

Notes

ℓ 1 **homeshare**「ホームシェア」持ち家のある高齢者や障がい者と、住居を必要とする若者とをマッチングさせるプログラム。若者は家主の身の回りの補助をしつつ、共に生活する　ℓ 2 **Two Generations**「ツー・ジェネレーションズ」ロンドンにある、高齢者や障がい者と若者とのホームシェアを斡旋する会社。2018 年設立　ℓ 11 **fuchsia**「フクシア」熱帯・亜熱帯気候の地域原産の、アカバナ科の植物。垂れ下がるように咲く花が特徴　ℓ 20 **King's College**「キングス・カレッジ」ここではキングス・カレッジ・ロンドン (King's College London) を指す。ロンドンにある国立大学で、1829 年に創立された　ℓ 36 **Shakespeare**「シェイクスピア」イングランドを代表する劇作家、ウィリアム・シェイクスピア (William Shakespeare, 1564-1616) のこと。エリザベス朝時代 (1558-1603) を中心に活躍し、『ロミオとジュリエット (*Romeo and Juliet*)』や『ハムレット (*Hamlet*)』など多数の作品を手掛けた

児童文学と異世代同居

　C・S・ルイス（C. S. Lewis, 1898-1963）のナルニア国物語（The Chronicles of Narnia）シリーズの『ライオンと魔女』（*The Lion, the Witch and the Wardrobe*, 1950）では、戦乱を避けて田舎に疎開したペベンシー家の4人きょうだいが、同居することになった老学者「学者先生」の古い屋敷にある空き部屋の洋服ダンスからナルニア国に入っていきます。フランシス・ホジソン・バーネット（Frances Hodgson Burnett, 1849-1924）の『秘密の花園』（*The Secret Garden*, 1911）では、イギリス植民地時代のインドで、官吏の一人娘メアリー・レノックスがコレラで両親を失って孤児となり、血のつながらない伯父に引き取られてヨークシャーの屋敷に住むことになります。ヒュー・ロフティング（Hugh Lofting, 1886-1947）の『ドリトル先生航海記』（*The Voyages of Doctor Dolittle*, 1922）では、靴屋の一人息子トマス・スタビンズが、動物と話せる医者であり、ナチュラリスト（博物学者）のドリトル先生の屋敷に、助手として住み込みます。いずれの物語でも、ファンタジーの世界の展開と並行して、異世代の交流が描かれています。

MOVING ON

Making a Summary

Fill the gaps to complete the summary.

An organisation called Two Generations aims to reduce loneliness by (**m**　　　　　) elderly people with a (**s**　　　　　) room with young people who need (**a**　　　　　) accommodation. Norman is an elderly person, whose wife died several years ago. When he needed company, he was introduced to George, a young Syrian man. George's family lives far away, so he (**l**　　　　　) feels he has no family except for (**v**　　　　　) communication by computer. However, he has a sense of family with Norman. Applicants are heavily (**v**　　　　　), and have to (**c**　　　　　) to six months or a year, but in fact George and Norman have been together for longer. Norman can feel safe as he has company at night, and (**r**　　　　　) his independence, while George gets free accommodation and company. George thinks Norman speaks like Shakespeare to him because he uses (**s**　　　　　) English, so he can learn from him. According to Norman, George's English is getting very good.

Follow Up

Discuss, write or present.

1. Take a look at the website (https://twogenerations.co.uk). What do you think of this scheme? Would it be successful in Japan?

2. Would you like to share a house with an elderly person in this way?

3. George said that he is learning English from Norman, because he uses "English that is standard English". What do you think he means?

Unit 5

Cornwall's Lithium Mines

現代社会に必要不可欠なとある金属への需要が高まるにつれ、イギリス国内でその金属を産出しようとする試みが行われています。一体どのようなことが行われているのでしょうか。ニュースを見てみましょう。

On Air Date   2 July 2021

STARTING OFF

Setting the Scene

What do you think?

1. Why do you think that the number of electric vehicles has been increasing in recent years?

2. Electric vehicles don't need petrol or diesel, but do you know what substance they need instead?

3. Do you know what it is like to work in a mine?

Building Language

Which word or phrase (1-8) best fits which explanation (a-h)?

1. soar   [   ]

2. extract   [   ]

3. abundant   [   ]

4. seep   [   ]

5. brine   [   ]

6. pilot   [   ]

7. inevitable [   ]

8. pointless [   ]

a. sure to happen; cannot be avoided

b. salty water

c. without any importance, meaning, or relevance

d. pass slowly or leak through a small opening

e. rise rapidly or increase in amount, size or volume

f. existing in plentiful, more than adequate, supply

g. take, pull, or draw out, usually with some skill or care

h. a preliminary trial or test before deciding to do something

WATCHING THE NEWS

Read the quotes, then watch the news and match them to the right people.

a. And to have that domestic supply on your doorstep, it makes sense to see this mine in, into production.

b. We should work towards a circular economy, where we just recycle the metals we use.

c. So could the answer lie deep underground in Cornwall?

d. ... and that's why there's the need to look for it in places that we haven't looked for it before.

(　)　　　(　)　　　(　)　　　(　)

Understanding Check 2

Which is the best answer?

1. This video looked at the mining of two metals: tin and lithium. Which one of the following sentences about these two metals is correct?
   a. Lithium exists just beneath the water table, but tin comes from much deeper.
   b. Lithium exists about a kilometre below the surface, but tin is only about 120m deep.
   c. Tin is abundant in the South West but lithium is rare.
   d. They stopped mining lithium decades ago, but they plan to start mining tin.

2. Why is the demand for lithium about to increase dramatically?
   a. Electric vehicle batteries require a very large amount of lithium.
   b. There are only two or three grams of lithium in a mobile phone battery.
   c. Australia and South America have no more lithium left.
   d. The world is running out of oil.

3. Which one of the following sentences best describes the opinion of the second man interviewed in the video?

a. If we want to hit the net zero target, we must immediately stop mining for these metals.

b. We have found so much metal in Cornwall that we needn't worry about recycling.

c. In the future we can recycle used metals, but now we must continue mining.

d. We can continue to recycle, but when the metals run out, we must open more mines.

What do you remember?

4. Why is tin important?

_____

5. How much of the UK's future lithium needs could be supplied by this company?

_____

6. According to Rebecca Morelle, why will mining have to be different in the future?

_____

Background Information

　イギリス政府は二酸化炭素排出量と吸収量を差し引きゼロにするというカーボン・ニュートラルを2050年までに実現することを目標としています。それに向けて、ガソリン車から電気自動車への移行が急速に促進される中、蓄電池に必要なリチウムの需要が高まり、供給が追いつかなくなっています。新型コロナウイルス感染症のパンデミックから回復する兆しがみられるにつれ、停滞していた電気自動車の売上が急増し、2022年に入ってからリチウムは高値を更新しました。主な産出国であるオーストラリアや中国では、パンデミックの影響によって労働力の確保に困難があるものの、できるかぎりの増産を図っています。

　元素記号表の3番目にあるリチウムは、オーストラリアでの採掘量が世界一で、次いで南米で多く採掘されています。2019年の世界トップ10のリチウム鉱山のうち、5つが西オーストラリアに位置し、その推定埋蔵量の合計は4億7,000万トンを超えていました。アメリカ合衆国でも鉱山が見つかっていますが、土地を買収して採掘に参入しようとする企業と、周囲の古くからの住民や、居住区のネイティブ・アメリカンなどとのトラブルも発生しています。

　リチウムイオン電池の発明、開発、商品化では、日本の研究者や企業が世界でも群を抜いて活躍しています。開発の大きな一歩は、1979年にオックスフォード大学のジョン・グッドイナフ（John Goodenough）教授と、現東芝エグゼクティブフェローで当時東京大学から留学中だった水島公一氏によって踏み出され、次いで旭化成フェローの吉野彰博士らが、白川英樹教授の研究を踏まえて試作しました。一方、独自のアプローチで西美緒氏らにより開発を進めていたソニーは、1991年、世界に先駆けてリチウムイオン電池を製品化しました。翌92年には旭化成が東芝との合弁会社を設立して生産を開始し、94年にはパナソニックらも参入し、20世紀の世界のリチウムイオン市場は日本製品が圧倒するものとなりました。2021年にはトップ10社中、7社が日本企業、2社が韓国企業、1社がドイツ企業でした。イギリスは韓国を筆頭にほぼ全面的に輸入に頼ってきましたが、ニュースにある通り、国内での埋蔵が明らかになったため、採掘への期待が高まっています。

参考
https://www.mining.com/web/top-bid-for-lithium-up-140-after-musks-insane-levels-call/
https://www.mining-technology.com/analysis/top-ten-biggest-lithium-mines/
https://www.power-technology.com/analysis/is-this-the-golden-age-of-battery-innovation/

 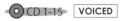
Watch the news, then fill the gaps in the text.

Newsreader: Now, with the rapid growth of renewable energy and electric vehicles in recent

years, it's no surprise that the demand for the metals that they rely on is

(^{1}). So could the answer lie deep (^{2}) in Cornwall?

Well, our science correspondent Rebecca Morelle takes a look.

5 **Rebecca Morelle:** Heading (^{3}) into Cornwall's South Crofty mine.

Richard Williams, Chief Executive Officer, Cornish Metals: Well, we're about 120

metres below surface right now. And we're actually beneath the (^{4})

water table. What you can see here is basically the sheet of mineralisation that was mined.

Morelle: Work stopped (^{5}) ago, but these caverns could soon open up again.

10 **Williams:** Anything with an electric (^{6}), a circuit board, whatever, has tin

in it. So, all of these objectives and uses that we are using to get to this carbon-neutral

(^{7}) require tin to some degree. And to have that domestic supply on

your doorstep, it makes sense to see this mine in, into production.

Morelle: Above ground too, new methods of mineral (^{8}) are being

15 trialled. Lithium, essential for batteries, is (^{9}) in the South West.

Morelle: This borehole reaches about a kilometre beneath my feet, where there are lithium-

rich rocks. And as the water down there washes over them, the mineral

(^{10}) out into the (^{11}). That's brought back up, and

I've got some of the liquid here. And it's from this, that the lithium is

20 (^{12}).

Morelle: The project is currently at the

(^{13}) stage. The

aim is to have it entirely powered by

renewable energy to make the

25 process carbon-neutral. Right now,

lithium comes from Australia and

South America. But the company thinks it could (^{14}) supply around a third of the UK's future lithium needs.

Lucy Crane, Senior Geologist, Cornish Lithium: A (^{15}) mobile phone battery has about two or three grams of lithium in it, whereas an electric vehicle battery can have up to about 50 kilos. So it really is this huge step-change in lithium (^{16}), and that's why there's the need to look for it in places that we haven't looked for it before.

Professor Richard Herrington, Head of Earth Sciences, the Natural History Museum: Two pieces of rock here that are both lithium ore- …

Morelle: The World Bank estimates we will need a 500% increase in the global (^{17}) of lithium by 2050.

Herrington: We should work towards a circular economy, where we just recycle the metals we use. But at this moment in time, we can't do that. It's just, the (^{18}) is too fast, it's too rapid. And to hit the target of net zero, we need those technologies now. So I think it's (^{19}) we will continue mining.

Morelle: But mining in the future will have to be different, to minimise and repair any environmental damage. Experts say a green revolution is (^{20}) unless the planet is protected in the process. Rebecca Morelle, BBC News.

30

35

40

45

Notes

ℓ3 **Cornwall** 「コーンウォール」イングランド南西端の州　ℓ5 **South Crofty** 「サウス・クロフティ」コーンウォールのプール (Pool) にあるスズと銅の鉱山。開発は 16 世紀に遡り、1998 年に閉山したが、新しい経営体制で再開発が行われている　ℓ6 **Cornish Metals** 「コーニッシュ・メタルズ」カナダのバンクーバー (Vancouver) で 2001 年に設立された鉱物採掘・開発を行う会社。2016 年にサウス・クロフティの採掘権を獲得　ℓ11 **carbon-neutral** 「カーボン・ニュートラルの」二酸化炭素をはじめとする温室効果ガスの排出量から、森林などによる吸収量を差し引いて、合計を実質的にゼロにすること　ℓ29 **Cornish Lithium** 「コーニッシュ・リチウム」コーンウォール西部のペンリン (Penryn) に本社がある鉱物探査・開発を行う会社。2016 年設立　ℓ34 **the Natural History Museum** 「ロンドン自然史博物館」ロンドンのサウス・ケンジントン (South Kensington) にある博物館。元々は大英博物館 (British Museum) の一部として 1881 年に開館　ℓ36 **The World Bank** 「世界銀行」貧困削減や開発支援を目的として途上国の政府に融資や助言を提供する国際金融機関。アメリカ合衆国のワシントン D.C. に本部がある。1944 年設立　ℓ42 **net zero** 「ネットゼロ」二酸化炭素実質排出量ゼロを指す

炭鉱のカナリア

「炭鉱のカナリア（a canary in a coal mine）」とは「警告」や「危険の前兆」を表す慣用句です。18世紀後半の産業革命以後、燃料となる石炭の需要が増加するにつれ、イギリスにおける炭鉱業は飛躍的に拡大しました。一方、炭坑での採掘作業は常に危険と隣り合わせで、有毒ガスによる中毒や爆発を未然に防ぐことが重要でした。そこで、イギリスの生物学者 J・B・S・ホールデン（J. B. S. Haldane, 1892-1964）の発案により、カナリアを連れて炭坑に入る方法が1911年から用いられるようになりました。カナリアの呼吸器官は高く飛ぶために多量の空気を取り入れる構造になっています。そのため人間よりもガスの影響を受けやすく、一酸化炭素など、無色無臭の気体の存在を知らせる検知器の役割を担わされました。炭鉱夫たちは籠に入れたカナリアの体調を見て、有毒ガスが流出しているかどうかを判断しました。また、カナリアが意識を失った際に蘇生できるよう、酸素ボンベつきの透明な箱型の装置に入れることもありました。ペットのように愛されていたとも言われる炭鉱のカナリアですが、動物愛護の観点から、1986年には使用が禁止されました。

MOVING ON

Making a Summary

CD 1-16

Fill the gaps to complete the summary.

In order to minimise the effects of climate change, there has been a rapid growth in (**r**) energy and electric vehicles. Therefore, the demand for lithium and tin, on which batteries rely, has been (**s**). Anything with an electrical connection contains some tin, so it makes sense to re-open Cornwall's South Crofty tin mine. At 120 metres below the surface, we can still see the sheet of mineralisation that was mined decades ago, and the (**c**) might soon open again. Also, a kilometre below, lithium is (**a**) all over the South West. Water washes over the rocks and the mineral (**s**) out into the (**b**). That liquid is then brought up to the surface and lithium is (**e**) from it. This project is now at the (**p**) stage, but eventually it is hoped that it will supply a third of the UK's lithium needs. One day, we might be able to recycle all the metals we use, but it is (**i**) that we will continue mining. However, if we don't minimise environmental damage, the green revolution will be (**p**).

Follow Up

Discuss, write or present.

1. Is there any lithium in Japan? Find out what countries produce the world's lithium.

2. In the UK, by 2030, no new cars sold can be powered by petrol or diesel. What do you think of this policy? Do you think it will succeed? Is there a similar law in Japan?

3. How do you recycle electronic goods in Japan? What are the rules, and do people obey the rules?

Unit 6

How to Be Happy on Blue Monday

緯度の高いイギリスでは、冬の夜長に気が滅入ることもあります。新型コロナウイルスの影響で、心がふさぐこともあるでしょう。そんな時に、活力を取り戻そうとする催しが行われました。どのようなものか、ニュースを見てみましょう。

On Air Date   17 January 2022

STARTING OFF

Setting the Scene

What do you think?

1. What is your favourite day of the year, and what is your least favourite?

2. What is your favourite colour, and why?

3. When you are feeling blue, what do you do to make yourself happy?

Building Language

Which word or phrase (1-8) best fits which explanation (a-h)?

1. depressing   [   ]

2. well-being   [   ]

3. struggle   [   ]

4. exaggerate   [   ]

5. beneficial   [   ]

6. gorgeous   [   ]

7. uplifting   [   ]

8. explore   [   ]

a. examine; investigate; look into closely

b. condition of being healthy, contented or successful

c. have difficulty in dealing with something

d. advantageous; good for you

e. describe something as bigger or more important than it actually is

f. wonderful; very beautiful

g. inspirational; offering hope and encouragement

h. causing a feeling of unhappiness and low spirits

Understanding Check 1

Read the quotes, then watch the news and match them to the right people.

    a. Hello, welcome to our Casa Chromatic.

    b. I'm at an amazing exhibition at the conference centre in St Pancras Hospital …

    c. So colour is something, it's actually a superpower.

    d. So, something that's trending on social media at the moment is Blue Monday.

( )   ( )   ( )   ( )

Understanding Check 2

Which is the best answer?

1. Which of the following sentences about Blue Monday is correct?

    a. Scientists have proved that it is the most depressing day of the year.

    b. On Blue Monday, it is always dark and cold outside.

    c. The idea of Blue Monday provides the chance to discuss mental health and well-being.

    d. The middle day of a pandemic is called Blue Monday.

2. Which of the following points about colour was <u>not</u> mentioned?

    a. It's free.

    b. We should appreciate the colour of flowers.

    c. Colour can boost your mood and lift your energy.

    d. Colour is like medicine.

3. What did Wendy Hurrell, the reporter, say calms her?

    a. connecting with nature

    b. looking at nice colours

    c. drinking a nice cup of tea

    d. a good sleep

What do you remember?

4. If somebody is struggling with mental health, what should they do?

_____

5. How did the curator of Casa Chromatic describe herself?

_____

6. How much does a conversation at the Theatre Cafe cost?

_____

Background Information

　「ブルー・マンデー（Blue Monday）」は1年で最も憂鬱な日とされ、通常は1月の第3月曜を指します。最初に提唱したのはイギリスの旅行会社スカイ・トラベル（Sky Travel）でした。もともと1月は、冬の寒さや侘しさ、クリスマス休暇が過ぎて日常生活が戻って来ることによる気持ちの落差などがあることから、1年の中で最も陰鬱な月とみなされていました。そこでスカイ・トラベルは、気分転換のために海外旅行を予約することを促すキャンペーンを企画し、人々が旅行を予約したいと思うようになる最適な日を割り出すよう、当時ある大学の非常勤教員で、現心理学者のクリフ・アーナル（Cliff Arnall）という人物に依頼しました。アーナルは、①天気の悪さ、②休暇中の散財による金銭の問題、③クリスマス休暇が過ぎてからの日数、④新年の抱負を断念してからの日数、⑤やる気の喪失の度合い、⑥行動の必要性を感じる度合い、といった様々な要因を考慮して数式を作成し、人々が最も憂鬱となる日を算出しました。その結果、2005年1月24日が最初のブルー・マンデーに指定されました。この数式には懐疑的な意見が多く、「最も憂鬱な日」が本当にあるのかどうかも定かではありませんが、以後、ブルー・マンデー自体は広く世間に知られるようになりました。

　今回のニュースでは憂鬱な気分を晴らすための催しが紹介されています。「カーサ・クロマチック（Casa Chromatic）」は、ロンドン中部および北西部国民保健サービス財団トラスト（Central and North West London NHS Foundation Trust）が支援する「アーツ・プロジェクト（The Arts Project）」の一環として開催された企画展で、精神疾患や薬物依存の治療に特化しているセント・パンクラス病院（St Pancras Hospital）にて2021年11月から2022年3月まで開催されました。また、自殺防止のために1953年から活動している慈善団体サマリタン協会（Samaritans）は、ブルー・マンデーにちなんだ「ブリュー・マンデー（Brew Monday）」キャンペーンを2017年から毎年行っています。2022年の催しでは、人気のコメディ劇団であるミスチーフ・シアター（Mischief Theatre）が協力し、ロンドンのシアター・カフェ（The Theatre Cafe）でコーヒーや紅茶を提供して交流するイベントを行い、劇場での上演やオンライン上でのストリーミング配信を通じて人々に笑いを届け、悩みを抱えている人々を支援するための活動資金を募りました。

参考
https://user.com/en/blog/blue-monday/#How_it_all_begun
https://www.candi.nhs.uk/news/casa-chromatic-art-exhibition
https://www.samaritans.org/branches/central-london/cls-news/mischiefcomedy/

Watch the news, then fill the gaps in the text.

Newsreader: Now, how are you feeling today? I ask because it is dark and cold outside, and

we are still in the (^{1}) of a pandemic. So, something that's trending on

social media at the moment is Blue Monday. It's supposed to be the most

(^{2}) day of the year. There isn't any science behind that, and many say

5   it's actually not helpful. However, it is perhaps an opportunity to discuss our mental

health and (^{3}). And Wendy has been in search of some simple ways to

(^{4}) our mood.

Wendy Hurrell: Well, a (^{5}) first of all. For those (^{6})

with their mental health, please talk to someone and seek professional help. It is there for

10   you. But, for a mild case of the winter blues, I've gone in search of a (^{7}).

Hurrell: And colour is key here. I'm at an amazing exhibition at the conference centre in St

Pancras Hospital, and here is the (^{8}).

Sue Kreitzman, curator, Casa Chromatic: Hello, welcome to our Casa Chromatic. My

end of year show is always about

15   colour. I am the Colour Queen of the

World. I'm not (^{9}).

Hurrell: And it makes you feel better. It

really does.

Kreitzman: It's, it's like medicine. It

20   really is. It's the best medicine, and it's oh, we have a sunny day today but often the days

are grey, and it gets dark very early. So come to my Casa. You will immediately feel

better.

Hurrell: One of the artists is quite the expert on how colour can be (^{10}).

Because, Momtaz, you have written a book on why and how colour (^{11})

25   us up. What's the reason for it?

Momtaz Begum-Hossain, modern colour theorist: So colour is something, it's actually a superpower. It's not just a (¹²   ) aesthetic. It has this incredible mood-boosting, (¹³   ) energy about all colours. And the great thing about colour is it's completely free and accessible for all.

Hurrell: These Samaritans have been at the Theatre Cafe this afternoon (¹⁴   ) Blue Monday into 'Brew' Monday.

Alastair Wallace, listening volunteer, Samaritans: People can feel (¹⁵   ) or sad or lonely on lots of days in the year, um, and you know, having conversations is a great way to help people start to feel better, to help people start to (¹⁶   ) some of those things. You know, it doesn't (¹⁷   ) anything other than the price of a cup of tea.

Hurrell: Connecting with nature always (¹⁸   ) me. Taking a moment to watch little garden birds. The BBC's *Winterwatch* starts tomorrow, so we could all join in.

Hurrell: And perhaps one of the simplest ways to (¹⁹   ) one's mood is to get out for a walk and talk with a friend, especially if the sun is shining. Wendy Hurrell, and Sonia Jessop, BBC London.

Notes

ℓ3 **Blue Monday**「ブルー・マンデー」憂鬱な月曜日。1月の第3月曜日で、1年で最も憂鬱な日とされる。2005年にイギリスの旅行会社スカイ・トラベルが打ち出した概念　ℓ11 **St Pancras Hospital**「セント・パンクラス病院」ロンドンのセント・パンクラス地区にある病院　ℓ13 **Casa Chromatic**「カーサ・クロマチック」手工芸会議所主催の色彩をテーマにした展覧会　ℓ30 **Samaritans**「サマリタン協会会員」イギリスの慈善団体「サマリタン協会（Samaritans）」の会員。心に悩みのある人や自殺を考えている人に、電話でカウンセリングやアドバイスをする　ℓ30 **the Theatre Cafe**「シアターカフェ」ロンドンのソーホー地区にあるミュージカルをコンセプトにした喫茶店　ℓ33 **'Brew' Monday**「ブリュー・マンデー」サマリタン協会が行っている、お茶を飲みながらおしゃべりをすることで憂鬱を吹き飛ばそうとするキャンペーン。brewとはお茶を淹れることを意味する　ℓ41 *Winterwatch*「ウィンターウォッチ」BBCの野鳥観察番組

イギリス国旗とナショナルカラー

イギリスのナショナルカラーは赤、青、白で、イギリス国旗にも用いられています。ユニオン・ジャック (Union Jack) として知られるこの国旗は3つの旗からできています。1603年、スコットランド国王ジェームズ6世 (James VI, 1566-1625) がジェームズ1世 (James I) としてイングランド王に即位すると、イングランドとスコットランドの旗を組み合わせた連合国旗が1606年に制定されました。イングランドの国旗は白地に赤い十字のセント・ジョージ・クロス (Saint George's Cross) で、赤い十字はイングランドの守護聖人である聖ジョージの血を表すと言われています。スコットランドの国旗は青地に白い斜め十字のセント・アンドリュー・クロス (Saint Andrew's Cross) で、スコットランドの守護聖人である聖アンドリューが処刑されたX字型の十字架を指すと言われています。その後1801年にイギリスがアイルランドを併合すると、アイルランドの守護聖人である聖パトリックに由来する白地に赤い斜め十字のセント・パトリック・クロス (Saint Patrick's Cross) が組み合わされ、現在のイギリス国旗が誕生しました。

MOVING ON

Making a Summary

 CD 1-19

Fill the gaps to complete the summary.

Blue Monday is supposed to be the most (**d**) day of the year, and it is an opportunity to discuss our health and (**w**). The reporter, Wendy, said that those (**s**) with mental health should seek professional help, but she had only a mild case of winter blues, so she went searching for a (**t**). First, she talked to the curator of Casa Chromatic, who said she wasn't (**e**) when she said she was the Colour Queen of the World, and colour was the best medicine. Momtaz is an expert in how colour can be (**b**). She thinks it is a superpower, with a (**g**) aesthetic and an (**u**) energy. And the great thing is that it is free and accessible to all. Next, the reporter met some Samaritans in the Theatre Cafe, where people can have conversations to (**e**) their sad feelings. Finally, Wendy said she was calmed by nature, and suggested one's mood could be lifted by going for a walk and talking with a friend.

Follow Up

Discuss, write or present.

1. Blue Monday is the third Monday in January. Why might that day be so depressing?

2. Do you agree with Momtaz about the power of colour? Do colours have the power to boost your mood and give you energy?

3. Do you agree with Wendy that connecting with nature and going for a walk is the simplest way to lift your mood?

Unit 7

The New Brixham Banking Hub

イギリスでは銀行が支店を次々と閉店させています。そうした状況下、銀行が無くなってしまったある町が、新たな試みを始めました。一体どのようなものなのでしょうか。ニュースを見てみましょう。

On Air Date   12 January 2022

STARTING OFF

Setting the Scene

What do you think?

1. How often do you go to a bank? Why do you go there?

2. If all the banks near you closed, would you find it very inconvenient?

3. How would it affect your town if there were no banks?

Building Language

Which word or phrase (1-7) best fits which explanation (a-g)?

1. transaction   [   ]

2. deposit   [   ]

3. withdrawal   [   ]

4. complex   [   ]

5. relieved   [   ]

6. juggle   [   ]

7. campaign   [   ]

a. funds which are taken out of a bank account

b. mix and keep several activities in progress

c. an act of business; buying or selling something

d. pleased; no longer worried or anxious

e. organise actions and speeches in support of something

f. funds which are put into a bank account

g. difficult or complicated

Understanding Check 1

Read the quotes, then watch the news and match them to the right people.

a. … obviously businesses run on cash, um, and cheques etc. …

b. This is also making sure that we can ensure there are financial services available …

c. Now they're hoping that it might turn into the bank hub.

d. … and you can go and have a conversation with them …

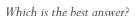

( )   ( )   ( )   ( )

Understanding Check 2

Which is the best answer?

1. What is a banking hub?
  a. It's a building that is shared by banks. They each use it one day a week.
  b. It's a truck in which a bank can move around the town and do business.
  c. It's a building where all the main banks can work together.
  d. It's a place where young people can train to be bankers.

2. In the video, a number of things that bank customers can do are mentioned. Which of the following was <u>not</u> mentioned?
  a. They can pay in a cheque.
  b. They can talk to a trained banker.
  c. They can withdraw and deposit money.
  d. They can borrow money to buy a house.

3. According to the businesswoman, why do small businesses prefer not to use the Post Office?
  a. They do not need to pay in cheques.
  b. The Post Office will only accept money in set amounts.
  c. It's not possible to juggle things around.
  d. Businesses don't use cash.

What do you remember?

4. Why is it necessary to open a banking hub in Brixham?

_____

5. Why is a local banking hub particularly necessary for the elderly?

_____

6. What is the local MP hoping for?

_____

Background Information

　イギリスでは、クレジットカードやスマートフォンによる支払いが普及して現金を持たない人が増えており、現金での支払いは全体の17%にすぎません。そのため、多くの銀行が支店を閉鎖しています。2015年から2021年にかけて、全体の半数に近い4,735支店が閉鎖され、その速度は加速しています。かつてはどの町においても複数の銀行が軒を並べていましたが、銀行の窓口やATMが急速に閉鎖し、とうとう支店が1つも無くなってしまった町もあります。ニュースで取り上げられているデヴォン州のブリクサムはその1つです。

　このような状況を受けて、イギリス王立芸術・製造・商業振興協会 (Royal Society for the Encouragement of Arts, Manufactures and Commerce) が調査を行いました。調査はアンケートとインタビューで行われ、現金のあり方を考察しました。その結果、現金を全く使わない人々がいる一方で、キャッシュレスに対して危惧を抱く人々がいる実態が明らかになりました。詐欺にあって不信感を抱く人や、銀行口座やインターネットへのアクセスのない人なども多く、社会全体で現金を廃止するにはまだ準備のできていない状態が浮き彫りになりました。街の小売商店も、4軒に1軒は現金取引が中心です。この調査結果を踏まえ、デジタル化への道を急ぎすぎることは経済への打撃が大きいと、協会は警鐘を鳴らしています。

　急速に進行するデジタル化に対応するため、協会は、①誰もが家の近くで現金にアクセスできるよう法制化すること、②給食や住民税などの基本的なサービスでは現金での支払いを受け付けること、③小学生から全ての学年でデジタル・マネーの授業を実施すること、④ブロードバンドの設置で取り残される地域を作らないこと、などの提言を発行しました。また、主要な銀行は有志の取り決めを交わし、支店を閉店する際には地域の現状を調査し、要望に応える努力をする態度を表明しており、その一環として「バンキング・ハブ」が構想されました。2022年7月時点では、試験運用されている2都市では2023年までの存続が発表され、ブリクサムを含む10都市で開設が決定しています。

参考
https://www.bbc.com/news/business-58245844
https://www.bbc.com/news/business-60879095
https://www.theguardian.com/business/2022/mar/23/lloyds-halifax-bank-of-scotland-shut-branches-england-wales-jobs-lost

Filling Gaps

Watch the news, then fill the gaps in the text.

Newsreader: Now, if you're missing being able to (¹   ) into your local

bank to draw out money or pay in a cheque, you're about to cash in. Brixham is to be one

of the first towns in England to open a banking hub, part of a new system set up to help

small towns (²   ) (³   ) the closure of their high street

5   banks. As Johnny Rutherford explains, it will mean customers and businesses of any bank

will be able to use it.

Johnny Rutherford: The busy town of Brixham, with its fishing (⁴   ),

small companies, and visiting tourists. But it no longer has a bank to help with the money

(⁵   ) of business.

10 **Councillor Paul Addison, Chairman, Brixham Town Council:** Brixham has a high

percentage of elderly population who don't necessarily have, um, internet connections or

acc-, easy access, (⁶   ) to banks in other towns.

Rutherford: This used to be Lloyds. It

was the last bank to close here in

15   Brixham last September. Now they're

hoping that it might turn into the

bank hub.

Rutherford: This is the bank hub at

Rochford in Essex. Brixham will have a (⁷   ) design run by the Post

20   Office, with staff from major banks helping out.

Cat Farrow, Cash Action Group: On one side you have a counter service where you can

carry out all your basic (⁸   ): your cash (⁹   ),

(¹⁰   ), cheque (¹¹   ). On the other side of the hub,

there'll be a private room where customers can talk to a trained banker from their own

25   bank. Um, and the banks with the most customers in that community, in Brixham in this

case, will take a day each to be in the hub and, and you can go and have a conversation with them about your more (^{12}) queries about your account

management.

Rutherford: Small businesses I spoke to today are (^{13}).

Liz Morton, YES Brixham: I think it's (^{14}) that we have a bank, um,

because obviously businesses run on cash, um, and cheques etc., so you have to be able to

go and pay those in.

Rutherford: Why not use the Post Office?

Morton: Well, the Post Office is difficult because they will only accept money in set

(^{15}), so, um, yeah, we have to (^{16}) things around

quite a lot.

Rutherford: Getting a hub and one of the first in England helped by (^{17})

from the town council, and local MP.

Anthony Mangnall MP: This isn't just about Brixham. This is also making sure that we can

ensure there are financial services

available in Totnes, in Kingsbridge, in

Dartmouth, in Salcombe, and across

the whole of the South West. Um, so,

I'm hoping if we can make a good

show of it in Brixham, we can, we can

(^{18}) it (^{19}) to other towns.

Rutherford: Final details are still in (^{20}), but I'm told the hub will be

open before the end of this year. Johnny Rutherford, *BBC Spotlight*, Brixham.

30

35

40

45

| Notes |

ℓ2 **Brixham** 「ブリクサム」イングランド南西部のデヴォン州にある町　ℓ13 **Lloyds (Bank)** 「ロイズ（銀行）」1765 年にバーミンガムで設立された大手銀行　ℓ19 **Rochford** 「ロッチフォード」イングランド東部のエセックスにある町　ℓ19 **the Post Office** 「ポスト・オフィス」イギリスにおいて郵便局の窓口業務を担い、切手販売や銀行機能などを提供している会社。1986 年設立　ℓ21 **Cash Action Group** (CAG)「キャッシュ・アクション・グループ」イギリスにおいて消えつつある現金へのアクセスを保証することを目指し、主要銀行やポスト・オフィス、中小企業連盟、消費者団体などから構成されたグループ。正式名称は The Access to Cash Action Group　ℓ30 **YES Brixham** 「YES ブリクサム」YES とは Youth Enquiry Service（青少年相談サービス）の略で、主に若者への支援を行っている慈善団体。YES ブリクサムは 1996 年に設立され、活動の一環としてチャリティー・ショップを運営している　ℓ41 **Totnes** 「トットネス」イングランド南西部のデヴォン州にある町　ℓ41 **Kingsbridge** 「キングスブリッジ」イングランド南西部のデヴォン州にある町　ℓ42 **Dartmouth** 「ダートマス」イングランド南西部のデヴォン州にある町　ℓ42 **Salcombe** 「サルクーム」イングランド南西部のデヴォン州にあるリゾート地として有名な町　ℓ48 **_BBC Spotlight_** 「BBC スポットライト」BBC サウス・ウェストによる地域ニュース番組。1961年放送開始

バンク・ホリデー

イギリスでは公休日を「バンク・ホリデー (bank holiday)」と呼びます。当初は 1871 年の「銀行休日法 (Bank Holidays Act)」で定められた銀行の休業日でしたが、銀行が休みになると金融取引ができなくなることから他の企業なども徐々に休むようになり、結果として国民全体の休日になりました。2022 年現在、イングランドとウェールズでは①元日 (New Year's Day)、②聖金曜日 (Good Friday)、③イースター・マンデー (Easter Monday)、④5 月初めのバンク・ホリデー (Early May Bank Holiday)、⑤春のバンク・ホリデー (Spring Bank Holiday)、⑥夏のバンク・ホリデー (Summer Bank Holiday)、⑦クリスマスの日 (Christmas Day)、⑧ボクシング・デー (Boxing Day) の 8 つを公休日としています。1 月 1 日の元日、12 月 25 日のクリスマス、12 月 26 日のボクシング・デー以外は年によって日付が変わります。また、日本の祝日のように、バンク・ホリデーが土日と重なる場合、通常は翌週の月曜日が振替休日になります。

MOVING ON

Making a Summary

 CD 1-22

Fill the gaps to complete the summary.

In the past few years, lots of high street banks have closed, so in some towns there is nowhere for people to carry out money (**t**   ). This is particularly difficult for elderly people, who might have no internet connection or means of transport. In Brixham, a fishing town, this problem will be solved by (**t**   ) an old bank building into a banking hub. Each of the main banks will be there for one day a week, and customers will be able to make (**w**   ) and (**d**   ), or pay in cheques. If they have (**c**   ) questions about their accounts, they will be able to talk to a trained banker. Small businesses are (**r**   ), as they run on cash and cheques, so they have to (**j**   ) things around if they use the Post Office, which only accepts money in set amounts. The local MP has been (**c**   ) for the Brixham banking hub, and he hopes they can (**r**   ) it out to other nearby towns to ensure there are financial services available there too.

Follow Up

Discuss, write or present.

1. Do you think the banking hub is a good idea?

2. All the banks in Brixham closed because of the effects of the internet. Has the same thing happened in Japan? What other shops and businesses has the internet affected?

3. The internet is being blamed for all these changes in the high streets. Why do you think the internet is having such serious effects?

Unit 8

Call to Clean Up London's Diesel Trains

イギリスは早くから自動車による大気汚染問題に取り組み、様々な規制を行っていますが、ある駅では列車による大気汚染が地域住民にとって問題となっています。何が起こっているのでしょうか。

On Air Date   23 November 2021

STARTING OFF

Setting the Scene

What do you think?

1. Is air pollution a problem where you live?

2. What damage is caused by air pollution?

3. What causes air pollution? Do trains cause it?

Building Language

Which word or phrase (1-7) best fits which explanation (a-g)?

1. toxic	[ ]	a. introduce slowly, or in stages
2. extension	[ ]	b. most important task to be done
3. palpable	[ ]	c. something that is a danger or risk
4. hazard	[ ]	d. rely or depend on
5. count on	[ ]	e. harmful, deadly, or poisonous
6. priority	[ ]	f. can be touched or felt
7. phase in	[ ]	g. something that is made longer or bigger

WATCHING THE NEWS

Read the quotes, then watch the news and match them to the right people.

　a. Chiltern railways acknowledges that air pollution is an issue …

　b. Any pollution is very dangerous.

　c. … electrification of the line is going to be very difficult.

　d. … and I'm not just complaining about my dry-cleaning bill.

(　　)　　　　(　　)　　　　(　　)　　　　(　　)

Understanding Check 2

Which is the best answer?

1. How dirty is the air in the streets around Marylebone Station?

　a. It's clear enough to see.

　b. It is not as bad as a dry-cleaning bill.

　c. The pollution is 80 micrograms more than the safe level.

　d. The pollution is ten times the safe level.

2. Which one of the following sentences about Marylebone Station is true?

　a. Electrification of the lines is expensive and not likely to happen soon.

　b. Battery-powered trains are being trialled and will soon be phased in.

　c. Air pollution is not an issue because it is not in a residential area.

　d. Diesel trains are not the only type of train to serve the station.

3. What does Councillor Rachael Robathan think will happen?

　a. Bridges will be repositioned.

　b. Switching to hybrids will be too difficult.

　c. The quality of the air will improve if they switch to hybrids.

　d. The line will eventually be electrified.

What do you remember?

4. Why did the second female resident mention her curtains?

_____

5. Why in particular does the male resident think that the air pollution is very dangerous?

_____

6. What are the two main challenges of the train companies?

_____

Background Information

　ロンドンでは、大気汚染に対する警戒心が強まり、交通規制を通して空気を清浄にしようという動きが高まっています。2003 年に渋滞緩和目的の道路課金である「渋滞課金 (Congestion Charge)」が導入され、指定区域の交通量は減少しました。また、2019 年には「超低排出ゾーン (the Ultra Low Emission Zone)」が定められ、排出量の基準を満たしていない乗用車には 1 日に 12.5 ポンド (約 1,875 円) が課金されることになりました。2021 年にはさらに区域が拡大され、当初は免除されていた地域住民も、所有する車両の排出量に合わせて課金の対象となりました。こうした車両への課金が補助金として支出され、自転車や歩行者のための環境整備や、公共交通機関の料金の見直しが実施されています。

　そのような中、ニュースにあるように、公共交通機関である鉄道では、ロンドン中心部の一部区間でディーゼル機関車が走行し、地域住民の懸念を引き起こしていました。ロンドンとバーミンガムをつなぐチルターン鉄道は乗客数の多い路線ですが、構造上電気化できない区間があり、ディーゼル機関車を使用していました。近隣のパディントン駅 (Paddington Station) で 2015 年に行われた調査では、覆いのある駅構内においてディーゼル機関車が発着するため、二酸化窒素、PM2.5、二酸化硫黄などの値が高く、イギリスでは規制がないものの、EU では安全基準に達しないほどでした。

　イギリス政府は 2018 年、ディーゼルエンジンのみを搭載した列車を 2040 年までに全廃するよう、鉄道業界に要請しました。2022 年 2 月、ディーゼルとバッテリーのハイブリッド車両がチルターン鉄道に登場し、今後車両数や走行地域を増やしていく計画が発表されました。これまで使用されていたディーゼル車両にロールス・ロイス社製のバッテリーが搭載され、時速 160 キロで走行できます。鉄道会社によれば、燃料消費率と二酸化炭素排出量は 25%、2 両編成で騒音が 75%、二酸化窒素が 70% 削減されます。環境を保護する為、あらゆる交通手段に変革が求められています。

参考
https://tfl.gov.uk/modes/driving/ultra-low-emission-zone/ulez-expansion
https://www.railway-technology.com/analysis/featurethe-big-stink-how-much-do-trains-really-emit-4807131/
https://www.bbc.com/news/uk-england-beds-bucks-herts-60331243

Watch the news, then fill the gaps in the text.

Newsreader: The recent (^{1} _____) of the Ultra Low Emission Zone has got

people thinking about the cars they drive, especially if they're diesel ones. But what about

trains? They also cause (^{2} _____), and some people living near Marylebone

Station say diesel trains are (^{3} _____) their health and their homes. Our

5 transport and environment correspondent Tom Edwards has been finding out more about

(^{4} _____) London.

Tom Edwards: A diesel train leaving

Marylebone Station this morning,

and you can clearly see the pollution

10 it (^{5} _____) out.

According to the Council, streets

nearby have ten times the safe

pollution levels.

Sheila de Souza, resident: That's 75 or 80 micrograms. That's twice the ...

15 **Edwards:** Residents are (^{6} _____) worried, and want changes.

Olivia Williams, resident: It is (^{7} _____). You can feel it in your throat. It

stings your throat when you breathe, it makes things dirty, and I'm not just complaining

about my dry-cleaning bill. If my lungs look anything like my curtains, it's a serious

health (^{8} _____).

20 **de Souza:** We're really, really (^{9} _____) (^{10} _____) the government

to put its money where its mouth is and actually clean up those trains immediately.

Roger Hart, resident: Any pollution is very dangerous. We've got schools nearby, we've got

a youth club right next to the station. Er, so it's, it's a real (^{11} _____) to us.

Freya Shanker, resident: I'd never walk along this road, full stop, because it's just too, it's

25 just (^{12} _____). But if I have to take the steps up there, then even going

along the foot bridge, it's, you know, just all the smoke is (¹³   ) into the road, and it, yeah, it's just (¹⁴   ).

Edwards: Marylebone Station is home to (¹⁵   ) routes into the Chilterns. It's also in a residential area and served only by diesel trains. Plans to (¹⁶   ) the lines would cost billions and aren't at the moment a (¹⁷   ).

30

Edwards: Chiltern Railways acknowledges that air pollution is an issue, but it says it is (¹⁸   ) to decarbonising its train fleet, and it's now trialling battery-powered trains close to stations like Marylebone. But, that could take some time to (¹⁹   ) (²⁰   ) if the trials are successful.

35

Edwards: The Council has also now written to the government, asking for changes.

Councillor Rachael Robathan, leader, Westminster Council: Because of the positioning of bridges etc., electrification of the line is going to be very difficult. But the switch to hybrids is (²¹   ) doable, and we'd just like to see a very clear timeline, so that we can (²²   ) exactly when this switch is going to take place, and the air quality will improve.

40

Edwards: All of this highlights the challenges: cleaning up and decarbonising transport networks while trying to maintain services. In the meantime, residents here say they're the ones (²³   ). Tom Edwards, BBC London.

45

Notes

ℓ1 **the Ultra Low Emission Zone**「超低排出ゾーン」ロンドン市内中心部に乗り入れる排ガス規制を満たしていない車両に対して通行料の支払い義務を課す区域。略称は ULEZ。2019年4月に導入され、2021年10月に区域を拡大した　ℓ3 **Marylebone Station**「メリルボーン駅」ロンドン中心部のシティ・オブ・ウェストミンスターにあるチルターン鉄道の始発駅　ℓ23 **youth club**「ユースクラブ」社会奉仕団体が教会などと共に運営している若者のためのクラブで、社会活動、スポーツ、娯楽などを行う　ℓ30 **the Chilterns**「チルターン」ロンドン郊外、北西部にあるチルターン丘陵 (the Chiltern Hills) のこと。全長74kmで、南西から北東方向に広がっている　ℓ35 **Chiltern Railways**「チルターン鉄道」メリルボーンをターミナル駅とし、バーミンガム、オックスフォードなどに向かう列車を走らせる鉄道会社。1996年設立　ℓ40 **Westminster**「ウェストミンスター」ロンドン中心部にある特別区

蒸気機関車トーマス

人気のテレビシリーズ『きかんしゃトーマス』(*Thomas & Friends*, 1984-) の原作は汽車のえほんシリーズ (*The Railway Series*) です。イギリス聖公会の聖職者ウィルバート・オードリー (Wilbert Awdry, 1911-97) が幼い息子クリストファー (Christopher Awdry, 1940-) のために作った機関車の話が元になっており、1945 年出版の第 1 巻から 1972 年の第 26 巻までをウィルバートが、1983 年の第 27 巻から 2011 年の第 42 巻までをクリストファーが手掛けました。第 1 巻『3 だいの機関車』(*The Three Railway Engines*) の主役はエドワード、ゴードン、ヘンリーで、トーマスが登場するのは 1946 年出版の第 2 巻からです。作中では蒸気機関車たちが活躍していますが、イギリス国鉄のディーゼル化推進に伴い蒸気機関車が徐々に姿を消していく時代を反映して、1958 年出版の第 13 巻『ダックとディーゼル機関車』(*Duck and the Diesel Engine*) には、いじわるな機関車のキャラクターであるディーゼルが登場しました。

MOVING ON

Making a Summary

 CD 1-25

Fill the gaps to complete the summary.

The air in London is (**t**   ) because there are so many diesel engines. For cars, there has recently been an (**e**   ) of the Ultra Low (**E**   ) Zone, which reduces the use of diesel. However, trains also cause pollution, and the streets near Marylebone Station have ten times the safe pollution levels. The pollution is a serious health (**h**   ), as there are schools and a youth club near the station, and one person says it is (**p**   ), stinging throats and making things like curtains dirty. The local people are (**c**   ) (**o**   ) the government to put its money where its (**m**   ) is, and immediately clean up the trains, but electrification is too expensive, and it is not a (**p**   ). Chiltern Railways is (**c**   ) to decarbonisation, and is trialling battery-powered trains, but it could take time to (**p**   ) them in, while still maintaining services. Meanwhile, residents want a timeline for switching to (**h**   ), and an improvement in air quality.

Follow Up

Discuss, write or present.

1. Are there many diesel trains in Japan?

2. In the video, we heard from a number of residents demanding action from the government to clean up their local environment. Would people in Japan complain in the same way?

3. The first woman said that the government should 'put its money where its mouth is'. What did she mean? In what other contexts might we say this about a government?

Unit 9

The Fair Shot Café

ロンドンの一画に新しいカフェがオープンし
ようとしています。ここで働く予定の新人ス
タッフたちには、ある特色があります。彼ら
の研修の様子を見てみましょう。

On Air Date   6 October 2021

STARTING OFF

Setting the Scene

What do you think?

1. Is it easy for you to find a job these days? What sort of job could you do?

2. If somebody is finding it difficult to find a job, is it possible to get any help?

3. What abilities and skills do you need if you want to work in a restaurant?

Building Language

Which word (1-7) best fits which explanation (a-g) ?

1. hospitality   [   ]

2. perception   [   ]

3. predominant   [   ]

4. vacancy   [   ]

5. rigorous   [   ]

6. disseminate   [   ]

7. tailor   [   ]

a. severe; very careful to be correct and following the rules

b. businesses that look after people, such as bars, restaurants and hotels

c. greatest, most important

d. distribute; spread widely

e. design something so that it perfectly suits somebody's needs

f. an unoccupied job or post; a position needs to be filled

g. the way in which we understand and interpret something

WATCHING THE NEWS

Understanding Check 1

Read the quotes, then watch the news and match them to the right people.

   a. Being able to work, to talk about going into work ...

   b. Many of the trainees say it's already changed their lives.

   c. We are giving them so many different types of qualifications to give them that competitive advantage.

   d. Thank you. Have a good day.

( )   ( )   ( )   ( )

Understanding Check 2

Which is the best answer?

1. What is special about the Fair Shot Café?

   a. It has excellent hospitality.

   b. Most of the staff have learning disabilities.

   c. It is the first cafe this year to open in London.

   d. It will change the lives of its customers.

2. Which of the following sentences is true, according to the video?

   a. Six per cent of the cafe's staff have learning disabilities.

   b. Eighty per cent of adults have paid employment.

   c. It is thought about 94% of adults with learning disabilities don't have paid employment.

   d. About 20% of the cafe's staff will find jobs.

3. For the next few weeks, what is one thing the cafe will <u>not</u> be doing?

   a. They will be trying to raise some more money.

   b. They will welcome their first real customers.

   c. They will be asking employers to think about the potential of their trainees.

   d. They will be looking for more people with learning disabilities.

What do you remember?

4. What is the story of Aya, the female trainee?

_____

5. According to the first cafe manager, what has the greatest effect on the trainees' mental health?

_____

6. According to the second cafe manager (sitting at the table), what message does the cafe want to disseminate among employers?

_____

Background Information

　学習障害（learning disabilities）は、特定の症状を指すのではなく、個人によって様々な症状があります。複雑な情報を処理すること、スキルを学ぶこと、自分のことを自分で行うことなどに困難を伴う場合が多く、学習障害があっても働き、資格を取り、独り暮らしができる人もいる一方、日々の活動に困難を抱え、サポートを必要としている人も多く存在します。イギリス全体では約150万人、成人ではイギリスの人口の約2.16%である110万人が学習障害を持っています。そのうち18歳から64歳の働く世代では、イギリス全体で約87万人が学習障害を持つと言われています。学習障害がある大人の65%が有給の仕事をしたいと感じているものの、6.6%しか有給職に就いておらず、さらに仕事を持つ人のほとんどが非常勤職であるというデータがあります。

　そのような学習障害を持つ人の状況に挑むべく、ウェスト・ロンドン・カレッジとフェア・ショット・カフェが協力し、職業訓練を行っています。ウェスト・ロンドン・カレッジは障がい者を隔離せずに社会参加を促す「インクルーシブ教育（inclusive education）」に力を入れ、個々の学習者の状況に応じた学習プログラムを提供しており、2020年にウェスト・ロンドン・ビジネス・アワードの年間教育・訓練提供者賞を受賞しています。訓練生は接客業で働きたいと思っている18歳から26歳の学習障害を持つ人々で、週のうち1日は大学で英語、数学、デジタル技術などの教育的な面を学び、他の4日はロンドンの高級ショップが立ち並ぶサウス・モルトン・ストリート（South Molton Street）にあるフェア・ショット・カフェで、コーヒーの淹れ方やレジ操作などの実践的なスキルを学びます。訓練生はバリスタや衛生の資格を取得できるだけでなく、その後の就業準備に必要な職探しや履歴書の書き方、面接の受け方なども学びます。毎年このプログラムでは、学習障害のある12人の若者に職場経験を11ヶ月にわたって提供した後、実際の職場で仕事を見つける手助けをし、就職後も最初の6ヶ月のサポートを行っています。訓練によって継続的に有給職に就くことを目指すこのプログラムは、学習障害を持つ人々の就業の可能性を広げる助けになっています。

参考
https://www.nhs.uk/conditions/learning-disabilities/
https://www.learningdisabilities.org.uk/learning-disabilities
https://www.fairshot.co.uk/

Watch the news, then fill the gaps in the text.

Newsreader: Next, a new cafe is due to open in London in a few weeks' time, run mostly by

staff who have (¹   ) (²   ). The people behind it say

they hope it will challenge (³   ) and help them get paid employment in

(⁴   ). Many of the trainees say it's already changed their lives. Sonia

5   Jessop has more.

Sonia Jessop: Today, they're training. But soon they'll be (⁵   ) real customers.

Geoffrey: Thank you. Have a good day.

Trainer: Amazing!

Jessop: The Fair Shot Café hasn't yet opened its doors, but its (⁶   ) are

10   getting ready at West London College.

Aya: What I like about Fair Shot Café is making different types of sandwiches, making the

coffees, and socialising with my (⁷   ).

Jessop: It'll be Aya's first job and she can't wait to get started.

Aya: I kept on getting (⁸   ) from retail stores because of my lack of,

15   because I had a lack of experience and, and coming here has gave, gaven, has made me

feel equal to society.

Jessop: Eighty per cent of the cafe's staff have learning disabilities. They also have skills,

dedication, and are (⁹   ) to succeed.

Abdul: I want to help people, I want to work hard. And that's what I'm doing. I'm very

20   happy.

Jessop: It's thought only around 6% of adults with learning disabilities are in paid

employment, so the college believes this new (¹⁰   ) could make a huge

difference.

Sue Jenkins, West London College: Being able to work, to talk about going into work, the

25   same as their brothers, the same as their sisters, the same as their neighbour, it, it's the

hugest (¹¹   ) to their mental health and their well-being. We have students now who were (^{12}) non-verbal: they're talking, they're,

they're beyond everybody's (^{13}). It is completely life-changing.

Jessop: The cafe's director hopes their first site in Mayfair will challenge

(^{14}). The aim is for staff to stay for a year, then they'll be helped into

  30

their next job, with the skills to fill some of those (^{15}) in London's

(^{16}) sector.

Bianca Tavella, Fair Shot Café: We are giving them very (^{17}) training.

We are giving them so many different types of qualifications to give them that

competitive advantage. So, I do hope that we can just, kind of, (^{18})

  35

the message amongst employers that to hire someone with a learning disability, um, is

taking on all of their (^{19}) gifts and abilities.

Trainer: Geoffrey, what's this called again?

Jessop: Training is (^{20}) to each staff member, from coffee making to

customer service.

  40

Geoffrey: Make sure they, they will be

welcomed. Make sure they, we are

treating them with respect and

manners too.

Customer: Thank you.

  45

Jessop: With just weeks till they welcome their first real customers, the cafe's still busy

raising (^{21}) and calling on other employers to consider the

(^{22}) of these trainees.

Newsreader: And good luck to them!

Notes

ℓ 9 **The Fair Shot Café**「フェア・ショット・カフェ」ロンドンのメイフェアにある、学習障害を持つ人々の職業訓練を行うカフェ　ℓ 10 **West London College**「ウェスト・ロンドン・カレッジ」ロンドンのハマースミスを拠点とする大学。2002 年、イーリング高等専門学校 (Ealing Tertiary College) とハマースミスおよびウェスト・ロンドン・カレッジ (Hammersmith and West London College) の合併により設立された。正式名称はイーリング、ハマースミスおよびウェスト・ロンドン・カレッジ (Ealing, Hammersmith and West London College)　ℓ 29 **Mayfair**「メイフェア」ロンドンのウェストエンド地区にある地域。ハイド・パーク (Hyde Park) やグリーン・パーク (Green Park) に隣接し、オフィスや高級店が立ち並ぶ商業地区として知られている

インクルーシブ教育

「インクルーシブ (inclusive)」は「包括的な」「包み込むような」という意味の形容詞で、対義語は「排他的な」「(特権階級などに) 限られた」「相容れない」を意味する「エクスクルーシブ (exclusive)」です。教育を受ける権利は普遍的な人権であるはずですが、かつて、障がいのある人などは、義務教育さえ保障されていませんでした。時代が進み、特別学校等に就学できるようになっても、障がいのない子供と分離されているために、同年代の子供たちや地域の大人たちと触れ合う機会を奪われ、学校卒業後の進路も非常に限られたものになっていました。そして障がいのない人たちも、障がいのある人たちの生活や思いを知る機会もなく、健常者だけに都合のいい社会を長年にわたって作ってきたのです。イギリスでは、1944 年の「教育法 (Education Act)」以来、医療の名目で特別学校が一般化しましたが、1981 年の教育法で、障がいの有無に関わらず共に教育を受けるインクルーシブ教育の実施が盛り込まれました。2006 年 12 月に国連で採択された障がい者権利条約の第 24 条には、誰でも「生涯にわたって」「地域社会の中で」教育を受ける権利が明記されています。

MOVING ON

Making a Summary

 CD 2-04

Fill the gaps to complete the summary.

It is thought that only around 6% of adults with learning (**d**   ) are in paid employment. A new cafe in West London, the Fair Shot Café, hopes to challenge (**p**   ) about such adults, and help them get jobs in (**h**   ). Eighty per cent of the cafe's staff have learning (**d**   ), but they also have skills and dedication. They are given (**r**   ) training, (**t**   ) to each staff member, so that they can (**d**   ) the message among employers that hiring someone with learning (**d**   ) means taking on someone with unique gifts and abilities. The students were (**p**   ) non-verbal, but the biggest, life-changing effect on their mental health is that they can work, and talk about work. One student, Aya, said she used to be (**r**   ) due to a lack of experience, but now she feels equal to society. The cafe is calling on employers to consider the potential of the trainees, who, after a year training, are helped to fill the (**v**   ) in London's (**h**   ) sector.

Follow Up

Discuss, write or present.

1. Do you think that you have the skills to work in hospitality?

2. The trainer said it was good that the trainees could talk about work. What do you think about that? Why is that a good thing?

3. If you were a restaurant manager, would you employ trainees from the Fair Shot Café?

Unit 10

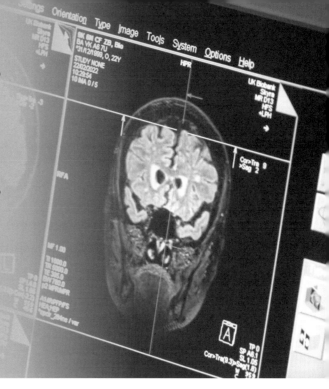

The Impact of Covid on the Brain

新型コロナウイルスに感染すると、人体には
どのような影響が残るのでしょうか。いまだ
後遺症についてはよくわかっていませんが、
研究者たちが脳に関する気がかりな結果を発
表しました。ニュースを見てみましょう。

On Air Date   7 March 2022

STARTING OFF

Setting the Scene

What do you think?

1. What are the symptoms of Covid-19?

2. What should people do if they think they have Covid-19? Do you think people obey the
   rules?

3. Are you worried about Covid-19?

Building Language

For each word (1-6), find two synonyms (a-l).

1. precise   [   ][   ]
2. reveal   [   ][   ]
3. assess   [   ][   ]
4. consequence   [   ][   ]
5. plastic   [   ][   ]
6. legacy   [   ][   ]

a. result	g. exact
b. evaluate	h. repercussion
c. pliable	i. report
d. estimate	j. endowment
e. resilient	k. accurate
f. gift	l. disclose

WATCHING THE NEWS

Understanding Check 1

Read the quotes, then watch the news and match them to the right people.

a. … changes in the brain of the participants who'd had Covid.

b. What smell training does is, it forces you to mindfully take in the smell …

c. … that's according to the latest research by Johns Hopkins University in the US.

d. The infected participants also had more difficulties, er, greater difficulties …

( ) ( ) ( ) ( )

Understanding Check 2

Which is the best answer?

1. Which sentence best describes the scientists' research plan?
   a. They were investigating the side effects of Covid vaccines.
   b. They were trying to find out exactly how many people have died from Covid.
   c. They wanted to know why Covid affected people's sense of smell.
   d. They compared brains of people who'd been infected by Covid with those who hadn't.

2. What did the scientists find out?
   a. People with mild cases did not lose their sense of smell.
   b. They discovered that 2% of people with Covid suffered from a shrinking brain.
   c. Covid causes the brain to shrink, and makes it harder to perform complex mental tasks.
   d. Memory improved if there was a loss of grey matter.

3. What is the purpose of smell training?
   a. It forces people to use their nose correctly.
   b. It helps people to regain their lost sense of smell.
   c. It stops people from losing their sense of smell.
   d. It trains people to find eucalyptus by smell.

What do you remember?

4. At the time of this video, how many people had already died from Covid-19?

_____

5. What are the scientists not sure about?

_____

6. Perhaps we need not worry too much about the brain shrinking. Why not?

_____

Background Information

　2020 年 1 月、イギリスで初めて新型コロナウイルスが確認されました。その後感染者の数は増え続け、2022 年 5 月時点における総数は約 2,200 万人で、感染による死者数は約 19 万人に上ります。多くの場合、新型コロナウイルスの症状は数日または数週間で回復しますが、中には数ヶ月にわたって後遺症が続く人もいます。その症状は極度の疲労、胸部の痛み、集中力や記憶力の欠如、不眠、関節痛、高熱、頭痛、嗅覚異常など多岐にわたるとともに、人によって症状も異なります。様々な研究が行われているものの、未だに後遺症については不明な点も多いのが現状です。

　新型コロナウイルス感染症を解明するべく、UK バイオバンクは大規模な研究を行いました。UK バイオバンクは、医学研究のため、人体に関する様々な情報を保管する目的で 2007 年に設立された世界最大規模のバイオバンクです。当時 40 歳から 69 歳のイギリス人ボランティア約 50 万人の身体検査結果や尿および血液サンプル、MRI などの情報を保有しており、その後最低 30 年間は追跡調査を行い、発病や調剤の履歴をデータベースに蓄積します。2022 年 3 月に科学誌『ネイチャー』(*Nature*) で発表されたこの研究では、UK バイオバンクに登録されている 51 歳から 81 歳のボランティア 781 人の脳の MRI を、新型コロナウイルス感染症が流行する前と後で比較しています。また、781 人のうち感染後平均 4.5 ヶ月が経過した 401 人と、非感染者 384 人の脳も比較されました。この研究では、脳の変化が嗅覚の異常に関連している可能性が指摘されています。もっとも、調査は変異前のウイルスと変異種であるアルファ株が流行していた時期に行われたものなので、オミクロン株等、比較的嗅覚の異常が少ないとされるその他の変異株でも同じ変化が起こるのか、今後の調査が注目されます。

　また、新型コロナウイルスに伴う嗅覚の消失に対し、その回復を目指す試みが行われています。ニュースで言及されているアブセント (AbScent) は創設者のクリッシー・ケリー (Chrissi Kelly) が 2012 年に感染症がもとで無嗅覚症になったことをきっかけに 2018 年に設立され、嗅覚異常の研究や嗅覚を失った人々のサポートを行っています。嗅覚異常はコロナ前でも人口の 5% である約 330 万人が患っていましたが、医療的な解決法が無いとされてきました。アブセントでは嗅覚異常を持つ人々に 1 日に 2 回、4 つ以上の香りを 20 秒ずつ意識的に吸い込み、それが何の匂いかを考えるトレーニングを最低 4 ヶ月以上行うことで、嗅覚の回復を促しています。まだまだ解明されていないことが多い新型コロナウイルスですが、今後の様々な研究によりウイルスや後遺症について明らかになっていくことが期待されています。

参考
https://www.yourcovidrecovery.nhs.uk/
https://abscent.org/
https://www.ukbiobank.ac.uk/explore-your-participation/contribute-further/imaging-study
https://www.bbc.com/news/health-60591487

Filling Gaps

Watch the news, then fill the gaps in the text.

Newsreader: Let's turn to the latest on the pandemic. Now more than six million people

have now died around the world after testing (^{1}) for Covid-19, that's

according to the latest research by Johns Hopkins University in the US. And here in the

UK a new study has found that even (^{2}) cases of Covid can cause

5   changes to the brain long term, as our science editor Rebecca Morell explains.

Rebecca Morell: We're starting to see the

(^{3}) impacts of Covid on

the brain as UK Biobank

(^{4}) the world's biggest

10   scanning project.

Woman: The task is about to start. If you …

Morell: Scientists have compared brain scans recorded before the pandemic, with images

taken after a Covid-19 (^{5}).

Morell: The scans (^{6}) changes in the brain of the participants who'd had

15   Covid. Almost all of them, 96%, had had a mild case. The researchers found that on

average the (^{7}) size of the brain had shrunk by up to 2%. There was a

loss of grey matter in the parts of the brain related to the sense of (^{8})

and (^{9}). And those who'd been infected found it harder to perform

complex (^{10}) tasks.

20 **Professor Gwenaëlle Douaud, the Wellcome Centre for Integrative**

Neuroimaging: These differences in the changes …

Morell: The scientists have been trying to (^{11}) what the changes mean.

Douaud: The infected participants also had more difficulties, er, greater difficulties, in

performing complex task, compared with those who did not get infected. And we can

25   relate that to how much of their brain had shrunk. Er, so yes, it does have, er, you know,

real life kind of, er, (^{12}).

Morell: What's not yet clear is whether the changes are permanent, or if they can be (^{13}).

Douaud: It can get scary to hear about the fact that your brain has shrunk. But we need to bear in mind that the brain is really (^{14}). By that we mean it can (^{15}) itself.

Morell: And there are signs this may be (^{16}).

Paola Totaro: No, it smells, smells like eucalyptus now, thankfully.

Morell: Paola lost her sense of smell after catching Covid in March 2020. Through smell training with the AbScent charity it's starting to get better. It's the olfactory part of the brain which is (^{17}) to smell that saw the biggest changes after Covid. The hope is, the brain can (^{18}).

Totaro: What smell training does is, it forces you to mindfully take in the smell, allow it to go back into your nose and then to think about what it is that you're smelling.

Morell: This study is just the start. It looked at earlier variants of Covid. It's (^{19}) whether Omicron would cause the same changes. The hope is further scans will help us to understand the (^{20}) left by Covid-19. Rebecca Morell, BBC News.

Notes

ℓ3 **Johns Hopkins University** 「ジョンズ・ホプキンズ大学」アメリカのメリーランド州にある私立の研究大学。世界有数の医学部を持ち、優秀な人材を数多く輩出している。1876年創立　ℓ8 **UK Biobank** 「UKバイオバンク」イングランド北西部、グレーター・マンチェスターに拠点を置く大規模なバイオバンク。バイオバンクとは、研究のための生体試料を保管する機関　ℓ17 **grey matter** 「灰白質」中枢神経系を構成する神経組織のうち、神経細胞体を含む部位。神経細胞体を含まない部位は白質（white matter）と呼ばれる　ℓ20 **the Wellcome Centre for Integrative Neuroimaging** 「ウェルカム統合神経画像センター」オックスフォード大学にある脳の神経画像を研究する施設。2017年、医学の研究支援を行っているウェルカム財団（the Wellcome Trust）からの資金提供により設立された　ℓ37 **AbScent** 「アブセント」嗅覚や味覚の疾患を持つ人々に対し、回復のための訓練を行っているイギリスの団体。2018年設立　ℓ45 **Omicron** 「オミクロン」新型コロナウイルスの変異株の1つ

ペストと英文学

　イギリスは1665年から67年にかけて、ペストの大流行やロンドン大火などの悲劇的出来事に次々と襲われました。ジョン・ドライデン (John Dryden, 1631-1700) は、長詩「驚異の年、1666年」('Annus Mirabilis 1666', 1667) において1666年を振り返り、より酷い事態もありえたものの免れたということを「驚異の年」という題名にあらわしています。ドライデンは疫病を避け疎開した先でこの詩を執筆しました。この時代に生きた官僚で、のちに海軍大臣となったサミュエル・ピープス (Samuel Pepys, 1633-1703) は暗号で日記を書きましたが、そこには当時の人々の暮らしが克明に記録されています。ダニエル・デフォー (Daniel Defoe, 1660-1731) も『ペストの年の日誌』(A Journal of the Plague Year, 1722) において、1666年のペストの流行を記録しています。デフォー自身は当時はまだ幼かったので直接経験してはいませんが、隣国フランスで疫病が流行った際、教訓のため、過去の伝聞から記録を残しました。

MOVING ON

Making a Summary

 CD 2-07

Fill the gaps to complete the summary.

　A group of UK researchers have been investigating the (**p**⁣⁣⁣⁣⁣) long-term impacts of Covid-19 on the brain. They have compared scans of brains after an infection with scans of the same brains before the pandemic. These scans (**r**⁣⁣⁣⁣) important changes, and scientists are trying to (**a**⁣⁣⁣⁣) what they mean. On average, the size of the brain shrank by 2% after a Covid infection, with most grey matter lost in the (**o**⁣⁣⁣⁣) part of the brain, which is linked to smell. This caused people to lose their sense of smell, but another (**c**⁣⁣⁣⁣) was that they found it harder to (**p**⁣⁣⁣⁣) complex mental tasks. As the brain is very (**p**⁣⁣⁣⁣), it might be able to heal itself, but it is not yet certain whether the changes are (**p**⁣⁣⁣⁣). However, loss of smell can be helped by smell training, which forces you to be mindful about a smell. It is hoped that further scans will help us to understand the (**l**⁣⁣⁣⁣) left by Covid-19.

Follow Up

Discuss, write or present.

1. Covid-19 often leads to a loss of smell. Do you think this is a serious problem? How would it affect you?

2. It appears that people who have been infected by Covid-19 find it harder to perform complex mental tasks. What sort of tasks do you think they mean? Is this a serious problem?

3. These scientists decided to research into the long-term effects of Covid-19. Do you think this is important? Do you think there are more important things to find out?

Unit 11

Women Learning Skills for Life after Prison

イギリスでは再犯率の高さが問題になっていますが、ある女性刑務所では、出所後の再犯を防ぐための取り組みが行われています。一体どのようなものなのでしょうか。ニュースを見てみましょう。

On Air Date   12 October 2021

STARTING OFF

Setting the Scene

What do you think?

1. Why do we send people to prison?

2. What do you think people do every day in prison?

3. What sort of problems do you think people have when they leave prison?

Building Language

For each word (1-8), find two synonyms (a-p).

1. inmate   [   ][   ]

2. evolve   [   ][   ]

3. collaboration   [   ][   ]

4. sentence   [   ][   ]

5. hone   [   ][   ]

6. bestow   [   ][   ]

7. ongoing   [   ][   ]

8. crucial   [   ][   ]

a. detainee	i. association
b. punishment	j. grant
c. develop	k. change
d. vital	l. partnership
e. give	m. improve
f. critical	n. unending
g. prisoner	o. sharpen
h. continuous	p. imprisonment

WATCHING THE NEWS

Understanding Check 1

Read the quotes, then watch the news and match them to the right people.

a. Just for them to know that they were doing something …

b. We are already acting on the mistakes that were made.

c. But since then, things have slowly got back to normal.

d. … I've sat with myself to say, what can I do to better myself as a person?

( )   ( )   ( )   ( )

Understanding Check 2

Which is the best answer?

1. Why did the BBC journalists and crew want access to Downview prison? What did they want to find out?
   a. why so many prisoners re-offend after they have left prison
   b. how prisoners design and make their own prison uniforms
   c. how prisoners with long sentences spend their time in prison
   d. how prisoners are being trained so that they can more easily find a job

2. In the video, we saw prison inmates doing three types of work. Which of the following was <u>not</u> mentioned?
   a. accounting and working with computer spreadsheets
   b. developing photographs, T-shirt and mug printing
   c. making personal protective equipment for hospitals
   d. stitching and drafting patterns for top designers

3. How many women find jobs within six weeks after leaving Downview prison?
   a. most of them
   b. about 10% of them
   c. none of them
   d. about one in five of them

What do you remember?

4. What does Michaela, the first prisoner we meet, ask herself?

---

5. What happened to make people ask questions about the quality of care for female prisoners?

---

6. According to the last woman (in a dark jacket), what is one of the things that they are struggling with?

Background Information

　イギリスでは女性刑務所の改革が進められ、出所後の社会復帰や再犯防止の取り組みが行われています。イギリスの司法制度の改革のきっかけとなったのは、2007 年に発行されたコーストン報告書です。報告者のジーン・コーストン女男爵（Baroness Jean Corston, 1942- ）は、2001 年から 2005 年まで女性として初めて労働党の議長を務め、枢密院の一員にも任命されました。議長を辞任後、コーストンは内務省の依頼を受け、イギリスの司法制度の下で弱い立場にある女性の調査を行い、報告書を出しました。その中では、社会への危険度や復帰の難しさや家族への影響など、様々な面で男女の受刑者には差があるため、それらを配慮する必要性を論じています。この報告書を受け、政府は社会や本人への影響を配慮しつつ、司法制度の改革を進めてきました。女性の犯罪は、万引きなど凶悪でないものが多く、犯罪者の中には、身体的・精神的な家庭内暴力の被害者も多く含まれます。また、子供を育てている母親が拘留されると、子供の犯罪率も上昇することがわかっています。このような事情を踏まえ、凶悪でない犯罪の場合はなるべく刑務所に送らず、コミュニティ・センターなどで対応する努力が求められるようになりました。

　そのような改革が進められる中、ヨーロッパ最大規模であるブロンズフィールド刑務所で、2019 年、女性入所者が独房で出産し、新生児が死亡するという痛ましい事件が起こりました。コーストン報告書では、妊婦はそもそも投獄されるべきでないとしており、すでにロシア、ブラジル、メキシコなど 11 ヶ国で実施されています。また、女性の入所者は精神的な健康面でも影響を受けやすく、2022 年には新型コロナウイルス感染症のパンデミックもあり、入所者の自傷・自害の件数が大きく増加しました。入所前にアルコールやドラッグに依存し犯罪に至る件数も多いため、依存に陥らないよう、予防策の強化が求められています。

　女性の入所率そのものは全体の 5% 程度の低い水準を保っており、再入所率も低いのですが、少数ながら同一人物が再犯を繰り返すケースがあります。前科者やホームレスなど、道を踏み誤ってしまった弱者を支援するため、ナクロ（Nacro）などの慈善団体が支援を行っています。困難は山積していますが、より安全で住みやすい社会を作るため、イギリスの司法制度は模索しています。

参考
https://www.theguardian.com/society/2022/feb/09/record-levels-of-self-harm-found-at-derbyshire-womens-prison-report
https://www.coventry.ac.uk/research/about-us/research-news/2022/new-report-recommends-legislative-changes-for-the-protection-of-pregnant-women-in-prison/
https://researchbriefings.files.parliament.uk/documents/LLN-2019-0095/LLN-2019-0095.pdf

Watch the news, then fill the gaps in the text.

Newsreader: Next, life inside one of the country's women's prisons. There are only 12 of them in the UK. We've been given rare access to one in Surrey, to see what's being done to try and cut re-offending rates by providing skills for a life after prison. Our home affairs correspondent, Lauren Moss, has an (¹   ) report.

5 **Lauren Moss:** Pinning, stitching, and drafting patterns for top designers: not the usual activities you'd (²   ) with a women's prison, but it's one of the courses run at Downview in Surrey, teaching qualifications that can be put to use when (³   ) are released.

Moss: Michaela's half way through a seven-year (⁴   ). She says she's using
10   the time to turn her life around.

Michaela: I definitely made a mistake and, you know, I personally do think I, I (⁵   ) to be here, and I've sat with myself to say, what can I do to better myself as a person? What can I do to, you know, grow and (⁶   ) and actually go out and, and have, you know, a successful career?

15 **Moss:** In (⁷   ) with the London College of Fashion, women spend four hours a day in the workshop, also (⁸   ) maths and English skills. During the pandemic, they made over 2,000 pieces of personal protective equipment for hospitals.

Winston Rose, tailoring tutor: Just for them to know that they were doing something, giving back to society, it was one of the greatest things they, you know, could have been
20   (⁹   ) on them at the time.

Moss: Across the quad, another group is developing photographs, T-shirt and mug printing, hoping to be ready to work in a Max Spielmann shop after prison.

Moss: Finding a job is one of the biggest challenges for ex-offenders. It's something Lianne, who's almost at the end of a three-year (¹⁰   ) is already focused on.

25 **Lianne:** I think it's good that they encourage people to be able to work on the outside. That was my main concern that I've always worked. I didn't want to go out and think, um, I've been, like I'm a (¹¹   ) now. I didn't want to, like, not be able to get a job on the outside.

Moss: Last month, questions were asked about the quality of care for female prisoners. A
30   report into Bronzefield in Middlesex found (¹²   ) failings after an

18-year-old gave birth on her own in a cell. Her baby died.

Moss: In her first visit here, the new Prisons Minister says such a thing can never be
(¹³   ) to happen again.

Victoria Atkins, the Prisons Minister: It is critical that those learnings from the report
are put into place. We are already acting on the mistakes that were made. A woman
should give, be giving birth in hospital, clearly not in prison. And, and the after-effects of
Bronzefield, I hope we're really going to see some (¹⁴   ). 35

Moss: Re-offending costs the UK 18 billion pounds a year. The minister hopes the workshops
will help (¹⁵   ) that.

Moss: Covid hit prisons hard too. At one point, 69 Downview staff were off and some had to
(¹⁶   ) roles to keep things moving. 40

Moss: In January there was a Covid outbreak here, and the majority of women had to spend
most of their time in the cells. But since then, things have slowly got back to normal.
Face-to-face visitation has (¹⁷   ), and activities have got back on track.

Moss: Seventy per cent of prisoners are on anti-depressants. Support for that and other health 45
needs is also (¹⁸   ).

Natasha Wilson, Governor, HMP Downview: It's about the quality of service with the
community. And making sure that, er, women are given the right, right health provision
because it's so (¹⁹   ) to the resettlement and re-integration. And that's
one of the things that I think we do struggle a little bit with at the moment. 50

Moss: Michaela's hoping to make a fresh start in the fashion industry when she's released.
With roughly just one in ten women employed six weeks after leaving Downview
though, finding work is an (²⁰   ) difficulty that both prisoners and MPs
say has to change. Lauren Moss, BBC London.

Notes

ℓ2 **Surrey**「サリー」イングランド南東部の州　ℓ7 **Downview**「ダウンヴュー」サリー州サットン（Sutton）にある女性刑務所。正式名は
「ダウンヴュー刑務所（HM Prison Downview）」。1989 年に男性刑務所として開設され、2001 年に女性刑務所となった　ℓ15 **the
London College of Fashion**「ロンドン・カレッジ・オブ・ファッション」ロンドン芸術大学（University of the Arts London）内の
カレッジの１つで、イギリスで唯一ファッションを専門とする大学。起源は 20 世紀初め頃に遡るが、様々な学校の統合が行われ、1974
年に現在の名称となった　ℓ22 **Max Spielmann**「マックス・スピールマン」イングランド北西部ボルトン（Bolton）に本社があるプリント
ショップ。2008 年設立　ℓ30 **Bronzefield**「ブロンズフィールド」サリー州アシュフォード（Ashford）にあるヨーロッパ最大の女性刑務
所。正式名は「ブロンズフィールド刑務所（HM Prison Bronzefield）」。2004 年開設　ℓ30 **Middlesex**「ミドルセックス」イングランド
南東部の旧州。1965 年にほぼ全域が大ロンドンに合併され、行政上の州としては消滅した　ℓ32 **Prisons Minister**「刑務所担当大
臣」司法省（the Ministry of Justice）に置かれている大臣

ロンドン塔の悲劇の王妃たち

　　テムズ河沿いに佇むロンドン塔 (the Tower of London) は王室所有の宮殿であり要塞で、かつては監獄や処刑場としても使われていました。16世紀の国王ヘンリー8世 (Henry VIII, 1491-1547) は6人もの女性と結婚・離婚または死別を繰り返したことで有名ですが、このうち2人がロンドン塔で命を落としています。2番目の妻のアン・ブーリン (Anne Boleyn, 1501-36) は、国王の愛人から王妃に成り上がり、後の女王エリザベス1世 (Elizabeth I, 1533-1603) を産んだものの、離婚され、反逆と姦通の罪を着せられて収監・斬首されました。また、5番目の妻でアンの従妹でもあるキャサリン・ハワード (Catherine Howard, 1521-42) も、やはり姦通を疑われて処刑されています。塔には幽霊が出るとの噂がありますが、失意のうちに亡くなった王妃たちの亡霊が彷徨っているのかもしれません。

MOVING ON

Making a Summary

 CD 2-10

Fill the gaps to complete the summary.

　(R   ) costs the UK 18 billion pounds a year, but finding work so that offenders won't return to prison is an (o   ) difficulty that both prisoners and MPs say has to change. Therefore, prison (i   ) are being taught qualifications that they can use when they are released. For example, in (c   ) with a London fashion college, women spend four hours a day in the workshop, (h   ) their maths and English skills. One woman, who was half-way through her seven-year (s   ), was pleased that she could (e   ) in prison to have a successful career, and another woman said she thought it was good that they are encouraged to be able to work, so they don't feel like (c   ). A man said that being able to give back to society was one of the greatest things to have been (b   ) on them. Support for depression and other health needs is also (c   ), and after an 18-year-old gave birth on her own in a cell, the Prisons Minister says the government is already acting on mistakes that were made.

Follow Up

Discuss, write or present.

1. In Setting the Scene, we discussed the problems that people have when they leave prison. But why do you think that so many of them re-offend and return to prison?

2. The video focusses on female prisoners in women's prisons. Do you think the story would be any different if we were discussing male prisoners in men's prisons?

3. The man said that one of the greatest things for the women was that they feel they are giving back to society. What do you think he means?

A Space for Green Businesses

ロンドンのとある共同ワークスペースに、同じ目標を持つ人々が集っています。新進気鋭の起業家たちの取り組みについて、ニュースを見てみましょう。

On Air Date   23 February 2022

STARTING OFF

▰ Setting the Scene ▰

What do you think?

1. The world's climate is changing. What kind of new businesses do you think we will need?

2. What challenges would these new businesses have?

3. What might be good ways to encourage and help these new businesses?

▰ Building Language ▰

Which word (1-7) best fits which explanation (a-g) ?

1. exclusively [　]

2. expand [　]

3. flush [　]

4. implicit [　]

5. derelict [　]

6. outstrip [　]

7. prolific [　]

a. clean something (e.g. a toilet) by washing through with a liquid

b. neglected, abandoned and unused; usually in poor condition

c. very productive; creating something fast and in large quantities

d. without actually saying so or using words

e. in a way that is limited to only one particular group

f. become greater or faster than something else

g. increase in size or extent

WATCHING THE NEWS

Read the quotes, then watch the news and match them to the right people.

   a. They're currently developing it with funding from Lambeth Council and Big Issue Invest …

   b. … other investors that are now coming in because they recognise the potential the space has.

   c. It's a fantastic experience to work with, li-, like-minded entrepreneurs.

   d. So climate change, um, is a much bigger deal than it was ten years ago …

( )   ( )   ( )   ( )

Understanding Check 2

Which is the best answer?

1. What is the purpose of the Sustainable Ventures workspace?

   a. to make sure that climate tech entrepreneurs can work in private

   b. to gather the best green brains so they can share resources and give each other advice

   c. to provide a place for businesses to work during climate change

   d. to provide a safe place for businesses to work during the pandemic

2. Where is the workspace that we see in the video?

   a. in the Shoreditch area, the centre of a lot of trends

   b. on the fifth floor of Lambeth Council, the headquarters of London power

   c. Thames Water, where demand will outstrip supply

   d. on a floor of County Hall, which has been almost derelict for 40 years

3. The video focused on three startup companies. Which one of the following did we <u>not</u> see?

   a. a company that designs toilets that use less water

   b. a company that will reduce the amount of single-use packaging

   c. a company that improves the efficiency of light bulbs

   d. a company that designs bricks to make homes more energy-efficient

What do you remember?

4. How many investments had Sustainable Ventures made over the previous four years, and what has happened from these investments?

_____

5. What is the future aim for the workspace we see in the video?

_____

6. What does the reporter think about the government's net zero plans?

_____

Background Information

　現在、二酸化炭素排出量削減という世界的な目標に向けて各国が努力し続けていますが、世界経済フォーラムの予測では、デジタル技術によって、世界での二酸化炭素排出量は 2030 年までに 15% 削減できる見込みです。気候テック (climate tech) とは、二酸化炭素排出量や温室効果ガス削減を実現しようとする技術のことで、それに関連する企業数は世界的に年々増加しています。また、気候テックへの投資額も増大しており、2016 年には 66 億ドル（約 9,240 億円、1 ドル＝約 140 円）、2019 年には 160 億ドル（約 2 兆 2,400 億円）、2021 年には 323 億ドル（約 4 兆 5,220 億円）という総投資額の推移からもわかるように、こうした企業への期待が年々高まっています。中でもヨーロッパでは投資が急速に伸びており、2016 年以来、投資額が 7 倍に増加しています。

　2019 年、主要国で初めて 2050 年までに二酸化炭素実質排出量をゼロ (Net Zero) にする法律を成立させたイギリスは、ヨーロッパで最も気候テックが発展しており、2016 年のパリ協定以来 416 社が起業しています。イギリスの気候テックへの総投資額は 2017 年に 1 億 3,800 万ポンド（約 193 憶 2,000 万円）、2018 年に 2 億 6,100 万ポンド（約 365 億 4,000 万円）、2019 年に 3 億 3,600 万ポンド（約 470 億 4,000 万円）、2020 年半期から 2021 年半期には 20 億ポンド（約 2,800 億円）と、ヨーロッパのどの国よりも多く、2013 年から 2021 年の投資額は、アメリカと中国に続いて世界第 3 位です。イギリスの気候テック関連企業は特にロンドンに集中し、ヨーロッパにおける気候テックの一大拠点となっています。

　ロンドンでの気候テックをサポートしているのが今回のニュースで紹介されているサステナブル・ベンチャーズ (Sustainable Ventures) です。2011 年に設立されたこの会社は、スタートアップ企業に投資をし、自社のリソースを提供することでその企業の成長を促すアクセラレーター・プログラム (accelerator programme) を運営しており、気候変動と資源の枯渇について取り組む 300 社以上の気候テックの発展を手助けしてきました。サステナブル・ベンチャーズのサポートは投資に留まらず、助成金申請の書き方指導や商業化に伴う手伝いなど多岐に渡ります。また、2015 年には、ロンドン・ブリッジの近くに最初の共同ワークスペースを開設し、その後カウンティ・ホールにも新たなワークスペースを設けて 109 もの会社を支援してきました。共同ワークスペースではワークショップなどのイベントが年 46 回開催され、気候テック会社同士のコラボレーションなどが生まれるきっかけとなっています。

参考
https://www.sustainableventures.co.uk/
https://technation.io/net-zero-report
https://dealroom.co/uploaded/2021/10/Dealroom-London-and-Partners-Climate-Tech.pdf

Watch the news, then fill the gaps in the text.

Newsreader: Next, the aim is to create thousands of green jobs. A new shared workspace

(¹   ) for startup climate tech entrepreneurs. It already

(²   ) 50 small businesses, sharing ideas from eco toilets to reusable

packaging. And there are plans to (³   ) further. Our work and money

5   correspondent, Marc Ashdown, went to meet them.

Agnes Czako, AirEx: We design smart air bricks to make homes more energy-efficient.

David Hollander, Propelair: We're trying to save the planet, one (⁴   ) at

a time.

Marc Ashdown: Just a couple of the 50 startup businesses sharing the Sustainable Ventures

10   office space.

Czako: It's a fantastic experience to work with, li-, like-minded entrepreneurs. You just bump

into each other in the corridor, you help each other with advice, you're sharing resources.

Ashdown: Everyone here has a climate tech or green focus.

Caroline Williams, junee: In the UK, we (⁵   ) 11 billion pieces of single-

15   use packaging, just from lunch on the

go, every year.

Mary Liu, junee: That's why we've

designed a borrow and return system

of reusable packaging.

20 **Williams:** We (⁶   ) last

year at a co-working space in the

Shoreditch area and we've been growing our restaurant and company partnerships in

central London.

Liu: Everybody sort of understands (⁷   ) a lot of the trends happening in the

25   sustainability space.

Ashdown: It's also (⁸   ) life back into County Hall. For 64 years the

headquarters of local London power, but for nearly 40 years now, much of the building

has lain (⁹   ).

James Byrne, co-founder, Sustainable Ventures: Particularly over the pandemic we've

30   seen, you know, changes in working (¹⁰   ), and it's worked really well:

we're well over full (ⁱ¹   ) here. So climate change, um, is a much bigger

deal than it was ten years ago when we first started. Um, and we're seeing

(¹²   ) growth in our businesses. Um, and the (¹³   )

drive is to, to kind of actually take some action and we're right at the heart of that.

Andrew Wordsworth, co-founder, Sustainable Ventures: Over the last four years

we've made 31 investments from a seed fund which makes us the most

(¹⁴   ) investor in the UK in climate change. For every pound we invest,

those companies have gone on to raise over £10 of further follow-on investment, both

from traditional climate change investors, but (¹⁵   ) from other, other

investors that are now coming in because they recognise the potential the space has.

Ashdown: Now this space is two (¹⁶   ) up, and it's three times the size of

the existing offices. They're currently developing it with funding from Lambeth Council

and Big Issue Invest, and the aim is to have a thousand businesses in here by 2025, making

it the largest climate tech (¹⁷   ) in Europe.

Ashdown: And it's all about (¹⁸   ), like this toilet, which uses just 1.5 litres

of water instead of the usual nine, the rest replaced with air.

Hollander: Thames Water say that by 2025 demand will (¹⁹   ) supply. Now

clearly they're working very hard to avoid that, but reducing the amount of water that

businesses use is a key way of helping to reduce water (²⁰   ).

Ashdown: The government's net zero targets are hugely (²¹   ). It's hoped

gathering the best green brains in one place will help rise to the challenge. Marc

Ashdown, BBC London.

35

40

45

50

Notes

ℓ2 **climate tech**「気候テック」二酸化炭素排出量の削減や地球温暖化対策のための技術　ℓ6 **AirEx**「エアエックス」気候テックや建設技術の開発を行っている会社　ℓ6 **air brick**「有孔レンガ」穴のあいたレンガ。空調や湿度の調整などの目的で、建物の壁面に使用される　ℓ7 **Propelair**「プロペレア」節水トイレの開発などを行っている会社　ℓ9 **Sustainable Ventures**「サステナブル・ベンチャーズ」環境保護に関連する事業を行う新興企業への投資や共同ワークスペースの運営などを行っている会社。2011年設立　ℓ14 **junee**「ジュニー」飲食店で客が持ち帰りの際に使用する容器の貸出システムを運営する会社　ℓ22 **Shoreditch**「ショーディッチ」ロンドンのイーストエンドにある地域　ℓ26 **County Hall**「カウンティ・ホール」旧ロンドン市庁舎。ロンドン南部のランベス特別区にあり、1922年から1986年までの64年間、庁舎として使用された　ℓ36 **seed fund**「シードファンド」投資家が、シード期（立ち上げの準備段階または設立後間もない段階）にある新興企業に投資する資金のこと　ℓ42 **Lambeth Council**「ランベス議会」ランベス特別区の議会　ℓ43 **Big Issue Invest**「ビッグイシュー・インヴェスト」社会や環境のための事業への投資を行う会社。ホームレスなどに雑誌販売の仕事を提供する企業ビッグイシュー（The Big Issue）から派生した。2005年設立　ℓ47 **Thames Water**「テムズ・ウォーター」大ロンドンやイングランド南東部のサリー州、南西部のグロスターシャー州などで公共用水の供給・処理を行っている企業

霧の都ロンドン

ヴィクトリア朝時代から 20 世紀前半にかけて、ロンドンといえば「霧の都」とロマンチックに呼ばれました が、実はロンドンの霧はスモッグで、大気汚染に他ならないことが徐々に知られるようになりました。 世界に先駆けて産業革命を成功させ、大英帝国を築き上げたイギリスでしたが、工場、自動車、蒸気機関 車、暖炉で燃やす石炭などの影響で深刻な大気汚染が進行していました。その頂点となったのが、1952 年 12 月 5 日にロンドンを覆った「ロンドンスモッグ (Great Smog)」です。現代の専門家によれば、この大気 汚染による死者は 1 万 2,000 人でした。日常的に悪天候だったため、スモッグに注意を払った地元民は当 初ほとんどいませんでしたが、午後になると空が次第に黄色がかり、腐った卵のような臭いが漂い始めまし た。翌日も視界は悪く、悪臭は 5 日間続きました。息もしがたく、同月 9 日には 15 万人もの人々が入院し ていたといいます。それから 60 年以上を経た 2016 年、テキサス A&M 大学の研究チームによる調査結果 が米国科学アカデミー紀要に発表されました。それによると、ロンドンスモッグの悪臭や空の色の異常、人 体への影響を引き起こしたのは、硫酸塩とよばれる硫酸の粒子でした。自然発生した霧の状況下、硫酸塩が 水滴のなかで二酸化硫黄と二酸化窒素の化学相互作用によって形成されたことが証明されたのです。

MOVING ON

Making a Summary

Fill the gaps to complete the summary.

A large office space (**e**   ) for startup climate tech entrepreneurs has been created in County Hall, which has lain (**d**   ) for nearly 40 years. Everybody in this sustainability space seems to understand trends (**i**   ), and entrepreneurs help each other with advice, and share resources. The space now hosts 50 businesses, and there are plans to (**e**   ) further. They have made 31 investments from a seed fund, which makes them the most (**p**   ) climate change investor in the UK. For every pound they invest, there have been ten pounds of follow-on investment, from investors who recognise the (**p**   ) of the space. One business designs air bricks, to make homes more (**e**   ). Another is designing a system of reusable packaging, and a third has designed a toilet that uses less water when you (**f**   ). That is very important, as Thames Water says that demand for water will (**o**   ) supply by 2025.

Follow Up

Discuss, write or present.

1. What do you think of this shared work space? Do you think that providing this space for climate tech companies will help the government achieve net zero targets?

2. They hope that the new toilet that uses less water will help reduce water consumption, but can you think of other ways to save water?

3. We have seen some ideas: more efficient toilet flushing, reusable packaging, and smart air bricks. Do you have any other ideas? Use your imagination!

Unit 13

Diversity in the Workplace

伝統的に階級の影響が強いイギリスで、この不文律に真っ向から向き合う大手企業が登場しました。その取り組みはどのような反響を呼んでいるのでしょうか。ニュースを見てみましょう。

On Air Date   9 September 2021

STARTING OFF

Setting the Scene

What do you think?

1. How easy is it to get a job in a top Japanese company? If you want such a job, what do you have to do?

2. Think of a successful Japanese financial or banking company that lots of people would like to work for. What sort of people do you think they would employ? What would be the best qualifications?

3. Do you think that it is easier for people from richer families to get good jobs?

Building Language

For each word (1-7), find two synonyms (a-n).

1. diversity   [   ][   ]
2. outcome   [   ][   ]
3. insight   [   ][   ]
4. aspiration   [   ][   ]
5. upbringing   [   ][   ]
6. mired   [   ][   ]
7. bias   [   ][   ]

a. caught	h. stuck
b. prejudice	i. variety
c. conclusion	j. ambition
d. childhood	k. understanding
e. wisdom	l. result
f. favouritism	m. dream
g. mixture	n. background

WATCHING THE NEWS

Read the quotes, then watch the news and match them to the right people.

a. So, it's already something quite hard to define …

b. And we want to reflect that, in, by reflecting society.

c. All the research and evidence shows that money really matters …

d. … the first big British business to set a specific target around social class …

( )   ( )   ( )   ( )

Understanding Check 2

Which is the best answer?

1. According to KPMG, who are 'working-class' people?

   a. people who work hard

   b. people whose parents do routine and manual work

   c. people who have not been well educated

   d. people with parents who are not rich

2. What is KPMG's target?

   a. Sixty per cent of middle-class people should be in a professional job.

   b. By 2030, about 30% of its top managers should be working-class.

   c. By 2030, most of its managers should come from the working class.

   d. They want to train drivers, plumbers, and farm workers to be accountants.

3. At the end of the video, Simon Jack suggests three reasons why KPMG is the first British business to set a social class target. Which of the following did he <u>not</u> suggest?

   a. Recently the company has been involved in a scandal, and this will help it to move on.

   b. It will enable the company to make more money.

   c. It is a good way to create a fairer and more equal society.

   d. Social class is difficult to define, compared to, for example, gender.

What do you remember?

4. According to the first woman, the Chair of KPMG, what is it in particular that leads to better results?

---

5. Why do they think that KPMG's attitude is not all about money? What else matters?

---

6. According to Reggie Nelson, why do some people like him feel uncomfortable talking about their upbringing?

Background Information

　イギリスの階級は、伝統的に①貴族や大地主等の上流階級（upper class）、②専門職や会社員などが属する中流階級（middle class）、③肉体労働や手作業に従事する労働者階級（working class）に大別され、裕福な上層階級と貧困にあえぐ下層階級の間には大きな格差がありました。しかし、これらの区分は時代と共に変化しつつあり、現在では社会的地位や収入といった面を考慮して分類されることが一般的です。個人の社会経済的背景（socio-economic background）は、2001 年から導入されている「国家統計社会経済分類（NS-SEC: the National Statistics Socio-economic Classification）」に基づき、収入が高いほうの親の職業によって定義され、8 つの階級に分けられます。社会移動性委員会（the Social Mobility Commission）は 2020 年、この 8 つの階級を、①大手企業 CEO、医師、弁護士といった「専門職ならびに管理職（professional and managerial occupations）」、②商店経営者、中小企業経営者、警察官といった「中間の職業（intermediate occupations）」、③受付係、電気技師、トラック運転手といった「労働者階級職（working-class occupations）」の 3 つに分け、16 歳以上の労働人口が属するグループの割合を発表しました。それによると、①「専門職ならびに管理職」グループに属する人は 37%、②「中間の職業」グループに属する人は 24%、③「労働者階級職」グループに属する人は 39% でした。

　現在のイギリス社会では、こうした階級の差がそのまま貧富の差となるわけではありません。例えば、中間の職業とされる事務職の平均年収は約 2 万 4,000 ポンド（約 360 万円）ですが、労働者階級である配管工の平均年収は約 3 万 2,000 ポンド（約 480 万円）となっており、階級が低いとされる職業に就いている人が必ずしも低収入であるとはかぎりません。一方で、階級意識はなおも根強く、受けられる教育に差が生じて就職活動で不利になる場合や、就職後も仕事内容や目指すことのできるキャリアに違いが生じる場合などがあり、社会全体における大きな課題となっています。こうした中、大手会計事務所 KPMG は 2021 年 9 月、上級職に就く労働者階級出身者の数を増やすことを目標とし、新たな採用プログラムの導入や、全従業員に対する社会経済的階級についての教育の義務化などを発表しました。その他にも、女性や少数民族、障がい者などの雇用を増やすことを目指しており、多様化を進めていく考えです。

参考

https://www.bbc.com/news/business-58485825
https://www.gov.uk/government/organisations/social-mobility-commission
https://home.kpmg/uk/en/home/about/our-impact/our-people/inclusion--diversity-and-equity.html
https://www.ons.gov.uk/methodology/classificationsandstandards/standardoccupationalclassificationsoc/soc2020/
soc2020volume3thenationalstatisticssocioeconomicclassificationnssecrebasedonthesoc2020

Watch the news, then fill the gaps in the text.

Newsreader: Now, the accountancy firm KPMG has become one of the first large UK businesses to set a target for the number of employees from working-class backgrounds. The firm has (¹   ) 'working-class' as people with parents who held routine and manual jobs, such as drivers, plumbers and farm workers. Our business

5   editor, Simon Jack reports.

Simon Jack: Getting through the door of top firms can be less about what you know, than where you come from. People from a middle-class background are 60% more likely to be in a professional job. KPMG has set a target that it wants nearly a third of its top managers to be from working-class backgrounds by 2030.

10 **Bina Mehta, Chair, KPMG:** So, (²   ) of perspective, (³   ) of thinking, (⁴   ) of (⁵   ) really does lead to better (⁶   ). And we want to reflect that, in, by reflecting society. And when I talk about working-class, I mean routine (⁷   ) and service organisations, so, the van drivers, the butchers, the factory workers. And that is the group of, um,

15   parental occupation that we want to increase amongst our senior colleagues.

Jack: Many office workers earn less than (⁸   ) on KPMG's list, which includes plumbers, so it's not all about money.

20 **Sarah Atkinson, Chief Executive, the Social Mobility Foundation:** All the research and evidence shows that money really matters, but so do (⁹   ), the environments in which you grow up, whether or not young people are (¹⁰   ) and recognised as being able to get into professions, top jobs.

25 **Jack:** Reggie Nelson was from an East End housing estate. He literally (¹¹   ) on doors until they opened. He's been at this money manager for three years.

Reggie Nelson: Where I grew up either music, football or crime was what people tend to do.

Jack: He said class was a tough issue to (^{12}).

Nelson: Not everyone is comfortable talking about their (^{13}), where they

come from. A lot of people might feel like, if they talk about their (^{14}) 30

then, in the environment, they might be seen as 'lesser-than' in comparison to their

(^{15}) that might have grown up in a middle-class or upper-class

background. So, it's already something quite hard to define, but also the conversations

can be quite awkward.

Jack: KPMG is the first big British business to set a specific target around social class, perhaps 35

because it's harder to define than (^{16}) or gender. It'll hope that more

(^{17}) means better financial (^{18}). It may also hope

that this will help turn the page after a period that has seen it (^{19}) in

accounting scandal, and seen the departure of its ex-boss, who said that training to

remove unconscious (^{20}) was a complete waste of time. 40

Jack: KPMG's move has been widely
welcome and it'll be interesting to
see if others now join them in what is
a comparatively new front in the
battle for greater (^{21}). 45
Simon Jack, BBC News.

Notes

ℓ1 **KPMG** 「KPMG」1870 年にイギリスで設立されたウィリアム・バークレー・ピート社（William Barclay Peat & Co.）を母体に、世界 154 カ国に進出している多国籍企業。会計監査・税務・経営コンサルティングを主力とする ℓ20 **the Social Mobility Foundation** 「ソーシャル・モビリティ財団」若者の社会的移動性を高めるために 2005 年に設立された慈善団体。高校生、大学生向けに、専門職に就くための様々なプログラムやネットワークを提供している ℓ25 **East End** 「イーストエンド」ロンドン東部地区。もとは低所得者層の住む地域 ℓ39 **accounting scandal** 「会計に関する不祥事」2018 年に大手建設会社カリリオン（Carillion）が倒産した際、それまで会計監査を担っていた KPMG の不正が発覚した事件 ℓ39 **the departure of its ex-boss** 「前社長の辞職」2021 年 2 月、500 名の社員が参加するオンライン・ミーティング上での不適切な発言を受け、当時社長だったビル・マイケル（Bill Michael）が辞職した事件

花売り娘から貴婦人へ

ジョージ・バーナード・ショー(George Bernard Shaw, 1856-1950)は1913年に発表した戯曲『ピグマリオン』(Pygmalion)で、当時のイギリスの階級社会に対する諷刺を描きました。作中で、言語学者のヘンリー・ヒギンズは、コックニー(Cockney)を話す花売り娘のイライザ・ドゥーリトルが上流社会から認められる英語力を身につけられるかどうかという賭けを友人のピッカリング大佐と行い、彼女の言語教育を開始します。コックニーはロンドンの労働者階級が話し、当時上流階級から批判を受けることが多かった英語です。ヒギンズの教育と自身の絶え間ない努力によって上流階級の英語を完璧に身につけたイライザは、身分を隠して参加した舞踏会でレディとして認められ、階級の壁を乗り越えることに成功します。この作品をもとにアラン・ジェイ・ラーナー(Alan Jay Lerner, 1918-1986)の脚本でミュージカル『マイ・フェア・レディ』(My Fair Lady)が作られました。1956年にブロードウェイで初演されたこの作品では、ジュリー・アンドリュース(Julie Andrews, 1935-)がイライザを演じてロングランヒットを記録しました。その後『マイ・フェア・レディ』は1964年にオードリー・ヘプバーン(Audrey Hepburn, 1929-1993)主演で映画化され、8部門でアカデミー賞を受賞する人気作品となりました。

MOVING ON

Making a Summary

CD 2-16

Fill the gaps to complete the summary.

KPMG is a very large British accountancy firm. It has decided that (**d**   ) of (**p**   ), thinking, and (**i**   ) leads to better (**o**   ). Therefore, it aims to have nearly a third of top managers from working-class backgrounds by 2030. By 'working-class', they mean people whose parents have routine and (**m**   ) jobs, such as drivers and plumbers. They hope they can turn the page, after being (**m**   ) in scandal, and an ex-boss who thought removing (**b**   ) was a waste of time. It's not all about money, as some working-class jobs are well paid, but it is also about people's (**a**   ) in the environment in which they grow up. For example, Reggie Nelson said that in his housing estate people just played football or committed crime. He had to try hard to get a good job, but can feel uncomfortable talking about his (**u**   ) because people might think he is inferior.

Follow Up

Discuss, write or present.

1. What do you think about KPMG's definition of 'working-class'? Do you think that you are 'working-class'? What about most of your friends?

2. KPMG are aiming for 'diversity', with employees from many different backgrounds. Are there any Japanese companies with similar aims?

3. The Chair of KPMG is a woman. Are there many leaders of Japanese companies who are women? Do you think diversity of gender is a good thing?

Unit 14

Repayment of Student Loans

イギリスでは学生ローンの返済方法をめぐ
り、改革案が検討されています。どのような
内容なのでしょうか。ニュースを見てみま
しょう。

On Air Date   4 October 2021

STARTING OFF

Setting the Scene

What do you think?

1. Why do so many people want to go to university?

2. How do students in Japan usually pay for their university fees? What about living costs, like rent and food? (Talk about your personal experience, if possible.)

3. Is it difficult for students to get by on a low budget? What do they have to buy? (Talk about your personal experience, if possible.)

Building Language

Which word or phrase (1-7) best fits which explanation (a-g) ?

1. leeway	[　]	a. large or good enough; not a level to be ignored
2. threshold	[　]	b. a compromise; a level where both sides benefit
3. demanding	[　]	c. an available amount of freedom to act
4. decent	[　]	d. difficult or challenging
5. pick up	[　]	e. pay; take on the responsibility for
6. penalise	[　]	f. the point, time, or level at which something starts to happen
7. balance	[　]	g. punish; make somebody pay, or put them at a disadvantage

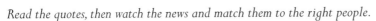

WATCHING THE NEWS

Understanding Check 1

Read the quotes, then watch the news and match them to the right people.

    a. Computer science and engineering are pretty popular subjects.

    b. … can they afford to start repaying their student loan as early as they might have to?

    c. How much they repay will depend on how much they earn.

    d. There's so much stress surrounding that because you need to pay your rent …

    (   )   (   )   (   )   (   )

Understanding Check 2

Which is the best answer?

1. How much do students have to pay at Staffordshire University?

    a. it depends on the subject: engineers pay more than digital artists

    b. more than £9,000, no matter what subject they are studying

    c. £27,000 a year for everybody

    d. £27,000 for computer science, but only £9,000 in the creative fields

2. How do students pay back their loans? Which of these sentences is correct?

    a. They must pay 9% of their income above £27,000 per year.

    b. They must start to pay back their loan as soon as they graduate.

    c. They must pay at least 25% of their loan back in full.

    d. They must pay all of their loan back within 30 years.

3. What happens to students who cannot pay their loans back because they are too poor?

    a. They are penalised.

    b. Their degrees are taken away from them.

    c. They only have to pay 50% of the total value.

    d. Their debts are paid by other people, who might not have gone to university.

What do you remember?

4. How is the government thinking of changing the student loan system?

_____

5. What does Vincent think about the possible changes, and why?

_____

6. Why does Emma think that fixing the threshold at £27,000 is a good idea?

_____

Background Information

　イギリス政府が大学生を対象として貸与しているローンは主に 2 種類あり、いずれも将来的な返済が必要です。授業料ローン (tuition fee loan) は、1 人あたり年間最高 9,250 ポンド（約 139 万円）まで借りることができる学費のローンで、各大学に対して直接支払われます。一方、生活費ローン (maintenance loan) は学生生活にかかる費用を賄うためのローンで、各家庭の収入や住んでいる場所に応じて貸与される金額が決まります。例えば 2022 年から 2023 年にかけての年度では、親と一緒に暮らす場合は年間最高 8,171 ポンド（約 123 万円）、親元を離れてロンドンで暮らす場合には 12,667 ポンド（約 190 万円）、それ以外の地域で暮らす場合には 9,706 ポンド（約 146 万円）まで借りることができます。

　イングランドでは毎年約 150 万人がこれらの学生ローンを利用し、約 200 億ポンド（約 3 兆円）が貸与されています。学生ローンを利用して 2020 年に課程を修了した人が抱える負債の平均は 45,000 ポンド（約 675 万円）で、働き始めて一定の収入を超えた時点から返済を始めることになります。返済計画は入学年度や地域によってあらかじめ決まっており、2012 年 9 月以降に入学したイングランドとウェールズ在住の学生の場合、年収 27,295 ポンド（約 400 万円）を超えてから、収入の 9% を返済に充てます。しかし、完済する人は全体の約 4 分の 1 にすぎず、2021 年 3 月末における未払いの額は 1,400 億ポンド（約 21 兆円）を超え、2050 年頃には約 5,600 億ポンド（約 84 兆円）まで膨れ上がることが見込まれています。こうした状況を打破すべく、政府は 2022 年 2 月、2023 年 9 月以降の入学者を対象として、返済開始の年収を 27,295 ポンドから 25,000 ポンド（約 375 万円）に引き下げる計画を発表しました。現行の制度では 30 年かけて完済する予定となっていますが、新しい計画では 40 年かかる見込みとなり、60 歳代までローンを返済し続けなければならないことになります。返済期間が 10 年延びることで利息の支払いも 10 年分追加されるため、対象年度以降に入学を予定している学生からは不満と不安の声が挙がっています。

参考
https://www.gov.uk/student-finance/new-fulltime-students
https://commonslibrary.parliament.uk/research-briefings/sn01079/
https://www.bbc.com/news/education-60498245

Watch the news, then fill the gaps in the text.

Newsreader: How much graduates in England need to be earning before they begin paying

back their student loans is currently being considered by the government. At the

moment, anyone earning just over £27,000 a year starts to repay their (**¹**   ).

But with only 25% of students expected to pay back their loan in full, there are

5   suggestions that the (**²**   ) could be reduced, so that more students start

repaying their (**³**   ). Our education editor, Branwen Jeffreys, has been

talking to students in Staffordshire.

Branwen Jeffreys: Growing up in Stoke, few go from school to university: half the rate of

(**⁴**   ) southern England, even though most graduates earn more.

10 **Jeffreys:** Students starting at Staffordshire

will all pay fees of more than £9,000,

from engineers who will earn high

salaries, to digital artists like Vincent

in his final year, who doesn't think

15 graduates should start repaying

earlier.

Vincent Althoefer, student: Computer science and engineering are pretty popular

subjects. So, I mean I think they're okay to maybe pay that (**⁵**   ), but

then, you know, for more of the creative fields, it can definitely be a lot more

20 (**⁶**   ), again because our salary is so low, starting out.

Jeffreys: Emma should get work straight away in (**⁷**   ), but says graduates

need a bit of (**⁸**   ) in the first few years.

Emma Baldacci, student: There's so much stress surrounding that because you need to pay

your rent, you need to pay, er, the bills, you need to pay for food, you might have a car,

25 insurance and then on top of that you need to pay your loan. And now, at this point,

obviously, you don't need to think about that until you earn 27K a year which is a

(⁹   ) amount of money a year.

Jeffreys: Today's students will repay their loans for 30 years after they graduate. How much

they repay will depend on how much they earn. And at the end of those 30 years, we all

(¹⁰   ) (¹¹   ) the bill for the (¹²   )

loans, whether we went to university or not. And that taxpayers' share of student loans

has now reached more than 50% of the total (¹³   ).

Jeffreys: When earnings hit just over £27,000, graduates repay 9% of income above that

(¹⁴   ). If it was lowered to 21 or 23,000, as some (¹⁵   ),

that would mean they start repaying sooner, and repay more.

Jeffreys: The Vice-Chancellor tells me it would (¹⁶   ) students getting a

degree later in life.

Professor Liz Barnes, Vice-Chancellor, Staffordshire University: If they're already

paying for a family, and paying for a

mortgage, can they afford to start

repaying their student loan as early

as they might have to? And so there

are (¹⁷   ) there.

But there may be a (¹⁸   )

we could have. We've been saying for some time now that maintenance grants are really

important.

Jeffreys: Despite the debate about cost, more students have chosen to (¹⁹   )

(²⁰   ) in England this year. Branwen Jeffreys, BBC News, Staffordshire.

30

35

40

45

Notes

ℓ7 **Staffordshire**「スタッフォードシャー」イングランド中西部に位置する州　ℓ8 **Stoke**「ストーク」スタッフォードシャーにある都市。正式名はストーク・オン・トレント (Stoke-on-Trent)　ℓ38 **Staffordshire University**「スタッフォードシャー大学」イングランド中西部のスタッフォードシャーにある大学。1992 年創立　ℓ45 **maintenance grant**「生活費補助奨学金」学生の生活費を補助する返済不要の奨学金

イギリスの大学と建築様式

「オックスブリッジ (Oxbridge)」とは 11 世紀に設立されたイギリス最古の大学であるオックスフォード大学 (University of Oxford) と 1209 年に設立されたケンブリッジ大学 (University of Cambridge) の略称で、両校とも多数の政治家や文化人を輩出する名門校として知られています。これら古い時代の大学は石造りのゴシック様式の校舎であるのに対し、バーミンガム大学 (University of Birmingham) やリヴァプール大学 (University of Liverpool) など、19 世紀後半から 20 世紀前半にかけて主要な工業都市に設立された大学群は赤レンガ造りの校舎だったことから「レッド・ブリック大学 (red brick university)」として知られています。さらに、ケント大学 (University of Kent) やランカスター大学 (Lancaster University) などの 1960 年代に設置が相次いだ大学群は、板ガラスなどを多用したモダニズム建築から「プレート・ガラス大学 (plate glass university)」と呼ばれています。

MOVING ON

Making a Summary

 CD 2-19

Fill the gaps to complete the summary.

If English university students take out a loan in order to pay their fees of more than £9,000, they have a (**l**⎵⎵⎵⎵) before they have to start repaying. They don't need to pay anything until their salary has reached the (**t**⎵⎵⎵⎵) income of £27,000, over which they repay 9%. If the debt hasn't been repaid after 30 years, they need pay no more, and taxpayers (**p**⎵⎵⎵⎵) (**u**⎵⎵⎵⎵) the bill. However, now, more than 50% of student loans are paid by taxpayers. In order to solve this problem, the government is suggesting that the (**t**⎵⎵⎵⎵) should be reduced to between £21,000 and £23,000. However, some students disagree with this idea. Graduates in creative fields earn less, and therefore repayment is more (**d**⎵⎵⎵⎵). Also, graduates have a lot of expenses, and it's good that they needn't worry about debt until they earn a (**d**⎵⎵⎵⎵) salary. Finally, the Vice-Chancellor said the suggested system would (**p**⎵⎵⎵⎵) older students, who might already be paying for a family. She agreed there were challenges, but there might be a (**b**⎵⎵⎵⎵).

Follow Up

Discuss, write or present.

1. What do you think of the idea that graduates need not start to repay their loans until they earn a decent salary? Would this scheme work in Japan?

2. Do most university graduates expect a higher salary? Do you think they deserve it?

3. The Vice-Chancellor mentioned students getting a degree in later life. Why would older students want to become students? Does this happen often in Japan?

Unit 15

Bringing Back Scottish Wetlands

スコットランドの海沿いの地域で、海面上昇を利用して環境問題に取り組もうという意外な試みが行われています。一体どのようなものなのでしょうか。ニュースを見てみましょう。

On Air Date   11 November 2021

STARTING OFF

Setting the Scene

What do you think?

1. How is the climate changing, and what are the main effects?

2. Is there anything that we can do about rising sea levels?

3. Are you worried about our future environment?

Building Language

Which word or phrase (1-7) best fits which explanation (a-g)?

1. significant   [   ]

2. irreparable   [   ]

3. breach   [   ]

4. diverse   [   ]

5. absorb   [   ]

6. reclaim   [   ]

7. emission   [   ]

> a. a discharge of something, usually a gas or liquid
>
> b. soak in or suck in
>
> c. cannot be fixed
>
> d. break through or make an opening in something
>
> e. important; worth paying attention to
>
> f. take back something that was lost, or convert it into something usable
>
> g. containing or including many different varieties

Understanding Check 1

Read the quotes, then watch the news and match them to the right people.

a. ... we need to be, er, you know, re-imagining our coastlines where we can.

b. ... but making space for natural stores of carbon, places like this that suck carbon dioxide out of the atmosphere ...

c. And at that point we kind of just stepped back and let nature do its thing ...

d. We will just perform a couple of experiments, using a couple of different machines ...

( )   ( )   ( )   ( )

Understanding Check 2

Which is the best answer?

1. How is this Scottish coastline being changed?

    a. The sea is being let back in and allowed to cover the land.

    b. Salt marsh plants are being planted on the land.

    c. The coastal defences are being strengthened to protect the land from the rising sea.

    d. The area is being re-engineered to bring back Scotland's coal mining past.

2. What do the scientists do with the cores of soil they take from the marsh?

    a. They put them in the museum at St Andrews University.

    b. In the laboratory, they examine the plant life they contain.

    c. They measure the different levels of carbon in the core layers.

    d. They wrap them in clingfilm and measure the amount of water in them.

3. What did Victoria Gill, the science correspondent, say about Grangemouth Refinery?

    a. The refinery is planning to slash emissions.

    b. The refinery is going to store the carbon that it produces.

    c. As the sea level rises, the refinery will have to close.

    d. Emissions from the refinery are balanced by carbon dioxide absorbed by the marsh.

What do you remember?

4. According to Victoria Gill, what is this marsh surrounded by?

_____

5. How has nature changed on the marsh in the past three years?

_____

6. What do the scientists say about the connection between climate change and marshes like this?

_____

Background Information

　2009 年、国際連合環境計画（UNEP: United Nations Environment Programme）は、森林などに蓄積される炭素であるグリーンカーボン（green carbon）の対語として、海洋生態系に吸収される炭素をブルーカーボン（blue carbon）と命名しました。ブルーカーボンとは、海藻や海草、植物プランクトンなどが光合成によって大気中から炭素を取り入れることで生成される有機炭素で、海洋植物の死後も海底の砂泥底に蓄積されます。これまでの二酸化炭素の吸収に関する研究はグリーンカーボンが主なものでした。グリーンカーボンは植物が無くなると炭素自体も無くなるのに対し、ブルーカーボンは植物が枯れても、何千年もの長期に渡って地中に蓄積されます。さらにマングローブの炭素蓄積量が森林の 10 倍であることなどが明らかになると、これまで遅れていたブルーカーボンに関する研究は、自然を利用した気候変動の解決策を模索している国々に注目されるようになりました。2016 年 11 月にパリ協定が発効した後、ブルーカーボンは一部の国で活用され始め、2017 年の国際連合海洋会議（United Nations Ocean Conference）では、マングローブ、海草、塩沼などのブルーカーボンの生態系を保護していくことに全会一致で合意しました。近年、ブルーカーボンの生態系を保護し取り戻すことで温室効果ガスの年間排出量の 3% が取り除かれるという研究がありますが、この数字は控えめな予測であるという研究者もおり、ブルーカーボンの可能性が期待されています。

　イギリスにおけるブルーカーボンの蓄積量については長い間過小評価されてきましたが、島国であるイギリスの 17,700 km の沿岸には塩沼や海草藻場があり、イギリスの年間炭素排出量の 2% を土壌に吸収することができます。今回のニュースで紹介されているスコットランドにはイギリス全体の塩沼の 13% にあたる 58.4 km^2 の塩沼がありますが、これまでにフォース湾（Firth of Forth）の 51% の塩沼が農業のための埋め立てや気候の変化により失われてきました。また、海面上昇が今のスピードで進行すると、スコットランド沿岸の資産のうち 12 億ポンド（約 1,800 億円）が 2050 年までに危機にさらされると予測されています。これらの塩沼を保護すべく、セント・アンドルーズ大学などの研究者たちが広大なスコットランド中の 47 の塩沼の土壌から 471 のサンプルを集め、塩沼の有機炭素量を測定する研究を行いました。その結果、スコットランドの塩沼全体では 37 万トン、1 m^2 あたりの平均量は約 6kg の炭素があり、地上の土壌よりも炭素量が多いことがわかりました。スコットランドではイギリス全体の目標よりも 5 年早い 2045 年までにネット・ゼロを実現することを目指しており、塩沼の保護や再生は温室効果ガスの除去や洪水の緩和、生態系の保護といった様々な観点から注目されています。

参考
https://blogs.gov.scot/marine-scotland/2021/09/14/new-study-into-significance-of-scottish-saltmarsh/
https://www.theguardian.com/environment/2021/nov/06/dangerous-blindspot-why-overlooking-blue-carbon-could-sink-us
https://data.marine.gov.scot/dataset/blue-carbon-stock-scottish-saltmarsh-soils

Watch the news, then fill the gaps in the text.

Female newsreader: Er, first though, rising sea levels, one of the most

(^{1}) (^{2}) of climate change, and causing

(^{3}) damage.

Male newsreader: However, a study of a restored coastal marsh in Scotland is showing there

5   could be some (^{4}), if rising water is managed properly. Our science

correspondent, Victoria Gill has more.

Victoria Gill: Digging into a changing environment. In an area that's surrounded by

Scotland's coal mining past and its

industrial present, there's a

10   (^{5}) happening

beneath our feet. Just three years ago,

this area was re-engineered to bring

the coastal wetland back to its natural

state.

15 **Allison Leonard, the Royal Society for the Protection of Birds:** You (^{6})

the coastal defences and let the water back in, but within a year or two we were seeing

salt marsh plants reappear. Um, we're now three years down the line and it's the salt, you

know it's all salt marsh. And at that point we kind of just stepped back and let nature do

its thing and we're really seeing the (^{7}) respond. So birds are using it

20   at high tide. You see lots of deer, hares in the spring.

Gill: As well as a (^{8}) wetland habitat this marsh has become a natural tool

in our fight to reduce (^{9}) of greenhouse gas into the atmosphere.

Professor William Austin, the University of St Andrews: OK, and a wiggle.

Gill: Marshland plants (^{10}) one of those key planet warming gasses, carbon

25   dioxide, which then becomes (^{11}) in the mud.

Austin: Yay! Whoof! That's a big one.

Lucy Miller, research technician, the University of St Andrews: This is some of the most, er, organic rich soils we've found in the, in the UK, compared to agricultural land, forest-, forestry land. So, we, we will, wrap this up in clingfilm, and um, just to keep it, hold its shape, and then we take it back to the University of St Andrews, we have a laboratory there. We will just perform a couple of experiments, using a couple of different machines, different equipment, um, just to kind of (^{12}) the different layers, um, different levels of carbon within the layers of the core here.

Gill: The scientists studying this site say it's (^{13}) a way to work with nature to manage one of the (^{14}) impacts of climate change: sea level rise.

Austin: I think there's, the (^{15}) of sea level rise are very serious and, er, we need to be, er, you know, re-imagining our coastlines where we can. And I think where there are (^{16}) opportunities, particularly for nature, that we should be thinking about, er, sea level rise as an opportunity for, er, coastal wetland habitat creation.

Gill: We can see a source of greenhouse gas (^{17}) from here, from the fossil fuel industry. There's Grangemouth Refinery just in the distance, and we still need to slash (^{18}), but making space for natural stores of carbon, places like this that suck carbon dioxide out of the atmosphere, will help us rebalance that.

Gill: Allowing the sea to (^{19}) this stretch of land has provided a glimpse of how we can help nature to help us (^{20}) the climate crisis. Victoria Gill, BBC News.

30

35

40

45

50

Notes

ℓ15 **the Royal Society for the Protection of Birds**（RSPB）「イギリス王立鳥類保護協会」鳥類や環境保護のための活動を行っている組織。1889 年設立　ℓ23 **the University of St Andrews**「セント・アンドルーズ大学」スコットランドのファイフにある北海に面した町、セント・アンドルーズにある大学。スコットランド最古の大学で、1413 年に設立された　ℓ45 **Grangemouth Refinery**「グランジマウス製油所」フォルカークにある町グランジマウスに位置する、スコットランドで唯一稼働している原油精製所。1924 年に操業開始

スコットランドの「生命の水」

　スコットランドはイギリスのほぼ3分の1の面積を占め、北海道と同じくらいの広さです。スコットランドの全面積の4分の3が、ヒース (heath) と呼ばれる荒涼とした野原や沼、石ころだらけの岩山で、農地としては不毛ですが、独特の景観が広がっています。デンマークのコペンハーゲンやロシアのモスクワと同緯度ですが、海流の影響で冷涼な西岸海洋性気候に属します。厳しい風土ですが、この荒地は泥炭 (peat) を堆積し、西風がもたらす雨雪が花崗岩に浸透し、泥炭層を抜けて、茶色い泥炭水 (peaty water) を作り出します。スコットランドを流れる川の多くが茶色いのはこのためで、この水がウイスキーを仕込んだり割ったりするのに最適なのです。夏と冬で温度差の少ない気候も、ウイスキーを穏やかに熟成させます。こうした風土の産物であるウイスキーの名前の由来は、ゲール語で「生命の水」という意味の「ウシュクベーハー (Uisge-beatha)」であると言われています。

MOVING ON

Making a Summary

Fill the gaps to complete the summary.

　Rising sea levels is a (**s**　　　　　) consequence of global climate change. A lot of the damage caused is (**i**　　　　　), but there might be some benefits if the water is managed properly. One example is an old industrial area which has been brought back to its natural state as a wetland, by (**b**　　　　　) coastal defences and allowing the sea to (**r**　　　　　) the land. After three years, it is all salt marsh, and has become a (**d**　　　　　) habitat: plants have reappeared, birds use it at high tide, and there are deer and hares in spring. Also, marshland plants (**a**　　　　　) the key greenhouse gas, carbon dioxide, which becomes buried in the mud. Scientists perform experiments on sample cores from the marsh, and have measured the levels of carbon in the layers. They say this (**r**　　　　　) a way to work with nature to manage the (**i**　　　　　) sea level rise, which can be considered an opportunity. Close to the marsh, there is a refinery, which is a (**s**　　　　　) of greenhouse gas (**e**　　　　　). We still need to slash them, but this new marsh sucks carbon dioxide out of the atmosphere, helping to rebalance it.

Follow Up

Discuss, write or present.

1. Reclaiming this marsh is considered to be a benefit because nature has returned. Do you think that this is really a benefit?

2. Are there any marshes like this in Japan?

3. Can you think of any other possible benefits of climate change?

BBC WORLD NEWS で

英語力につながる
ニュース習慣

なぜBBCワールドニュースで国際ニュースを見るべき？

24時間365日、世界中のニュースの現場から最新情報をお届け

世界中で起きている政治・経済・ビジネスなどのあらゆるニュースをリアルタイムでいち早く放送しています。

世界各国のジャーナリストが届ける、生きた英語

どの国際ニュース放送局より多くの国にジャーナリストを配置しているBBCならではの、様々なアクセントによる生の声をお届けしています。

BBCは世界で最も信頼されているニュースブランド

メディアの信頼性が問われる今、BBCは公平中立な報道を何より優先しています。

そのほか、様々なデジタルライブストリーミングサービスや多チャンネルサービスを通してご視聴いただけます。

詳しい視聴方法はこちらから

| BBC ワールドニュース | 🔍 |

最新ニュースはBBCニュース日本語版でもご覧いただけます。

    @bbcnewsjapan

BBC World News is a trademark of the British Broadcasting Corporation, ©BBC 2022

このテキストのメインページ
www.kinsei-do.co.jp/plusmedia/41

次のページの QR コードを読み取ると
直接ページにジャンプできます

オンライン映像配信サービス「plus⁺Media」について

本テキストの映像は plus⁺Media ページ（www.kinsei-do.co.jp/plusmedia）から、ストリーミング再生でご利用いただけます。手順は以下に従ってください。

ログイン

●ご利用には、ログインが必要です。
サイトのログインページ（www.kinsei-do.co.jp/plusmedia/login）へ行き、plus⁺Media パスワード（次のページのシールをはがしたあとに印字されている数字とアルファベット）を入力します。

●パスワードは各テキストにつき1つです。
有効期限は、<u>はじめてログインした時点から1年間</u>になります。

ログインページ

[利用方法]

次のページにある QR コード、もしくは plus⁺Media トップページ（www.kinsei-do.co.jp/plusmedia）から該当するテキストを選んで、そのテキストのメインページにジャンプしてください。

メニューページ　　　　再生画面

plus⁺Media トップ　　　メインページ

「Video」「Audio」をタッチすると、それぞれのメニューページにジャンプしますので、そこから該当する項目を選べば、ストリーミングが開始されます。

[推奨環境]

iOS (iPhone, iPad)	OS: iOS 12 以降 ブラウザ：標準ブラウザ	Android	OS: Android 6 以降 ブラウザ：標準ブラウザ、Chrome
PC	OS: Windows 7/8/8.1/10, MacOS X　ブラウザ: Internet Explorer 10/11, Microsoft Edge, Firefox 48以降, Chrome 53以降, Safari		

※最新の推奨環境についてはウェブサイトをご確認ください。
※上記の推奨環境を満たしている場合でも、機種によってはご利用いただけない場合もあります。また、推奨環境は技術動向等により変更される場合があります。予めご了承ください。

このシールをはがすと
plus⁺Media 利用のための
パスワードが
記載されています。

一度はがすと元に戻すことは
できませんのでご注意下さい。

◀ ここからはがして下さい

4172 British News
Update 5
(BBC)

plus⁺Media

本書にはCD（別売）があります

British News Update 5
映像で学ぶ　イギリス公共放送の最新ニュース 5

2023年 1 月20日　初版第 1 刷発行
2024年 9 月20日　初版第 4 刷発行

編著者　Timothy Knowles

田　中　みんね

中　村　美帆子

馬　上　紗矢香

発行者　　福　岡　正　人

発行所　　　株式会社　金星堂
（〒101-0051）東京都千代田区神田神保町 3-21
Tel. (03)3263-3828 （営業部）
(03)3263-3997 （編集部）
Fax (03)3263-0716
https://www.kinsei-do.co.jp

編集担当　戸田浩平・長島吉成　　　　　Printed in Japan
印刷所・製本所／三美印刷株式会社

本書の無断複製・複写は著作権法上での例外を除き禁じられて
います。本書を代行業者等の第三者に依頼してスキャンやデジ
タル化することは、たとえ個人や家庭内での利用であっても認
められておりません。
落丁・乱丁本はお取り替えいたします。

ISBN978-4-7647-4172-0 C1082